ROBERT ICKE

Robert Icke is a writer and director. His recent productions include *Judas*, *Children of Nora* and *Oedipus* at Internationaal Theater Amsterdam; *Enemy of the People* (Park Avenue Armory); *Animal Farm* (UK tour); *Ivanov* (Schauspiel Stuttgart); and *The Doctor* (Park Avenue Armory, Adelaide Festival, Almeida, West End and Burgtheater, Vienna).

His work while Associate Director at the Almeida (2013–19) included adapting and directing *The Wild Duck*, *Mary Stuart* (also West End and UK tour), *Uncle Vanya*, *Oresteia* (also West End and Park Avenue Armory) and *1984* (co-created with Duncan Macmillan, also Broadway, West End, UK and international tours). As a director, his productions included *Hamlet* (also West End, BBC2 and Park Avenue Armory), *The Fever* and *Mr Burns*.

His awards include two Evening Standard Awards for Best Director, the Critics' Circle Award, the Kurt Hübner Award for his debut production in Germany, and the Olivier Award for Best Director for *Oresteia*, of which he is the youngest-ever winner. He is a Fellow of the Royal Society of Literature.

William Shakespeare

PLAYER KINGS

adapted from Henry IV Parts One & Two *by*

Robert Icke

edition prepared by Lizzie Manwaring and Jack Bradfield

NICK HERN BOOKS

London

www.nickhernbooks.co.uk

A Nick Hern Book

Player Kings first published in Great Britain as a paperback original in 2024 by Nick Hern Books Limited, The Glasshouse, 49a Goldhawk Road, London W12 8QP

Player Kings copyright © 2024 Robert Icke
Introduction copyright © 2024 Robert Icke

Robert Icke has asserted his moral right to be identified as the author of this work

Cover photography by Miles Aldridge

Designed and typeset by Nick Hern Books, London
Printed in the UK by Mimeo Ltd, Huntingdon, Cambridgeshire PE29 6XX

A CIP catalogue record for this book is available from the British Library

ISBN   978 1 83904 358 1

www.nickhernbooks.co.uk/environmental-policy

INTRODUCTION

Henry IV Part 1 seems to date from around 1598, the year when it was entered into the Stationers' Register, and the year it was first published in a single (quarto) edition. That five more quarto editions were published between then and 1623 tells us something about quite how popular it was in its day. It's likely that *Part 2* was written within a year, and was printed in quarto in 1600.

Shakespeare took his history from *Holinshed's Chronicles* and, as he usually did, changed it to suit his purposes. He rearranges dates and facts, adds characters and sometimes bends them into his pattern: Hotspur, in reality, was no young rival, but twenty-four years older than Hal.

Again and again within the plays, characters change and retell action we've witnessed to suit their own purposes. Falstaff's fear of Hotspur's dead body, and his worry that he too might 'rise', blossom into a full-blown account of a Falstaff–Hotspur duel, fought for 'a long hour by Shrewsbury clock' (which we – and Hal – know simply didn't happen). Similarly, Hal's story to his father – of what he was thinking when he took the crown from the royal pillow – does not precisely report what we have previously heard him say. This, perhaps, is history in action, a reminder that a historical account is really only one person's story, after the event.

Sometimes the retelling precedes the event itself. Hal and Falstaff rehearse a conflict between Hal and his father, so that Hal can 'practise an answer' to his father's complaints. But when the player king is deposed and Hal takes the throne, his role as his father seems to evaporate, the play exposing some of the bloodier extremes of his relationship with Falstaff. He can, in his pretend role as king, be (as he later promises his father) 'more myself'. And what the real father–son conflict looks like, when we see it in a later scene, is something altogether different. Fathers – adopted, played, embodied, impersonated – are everywhere: even a wish can be a 'father to [a] thought'.

Hal's two father figures are only one of a series of mirrored pairs that structure the plays. There are two young rivals (Harries Percy and Monmouth), there are two rebellions, two justices of the peace, two kings (one holds court at the Boar's Head Tavern and, unlike the one in Westminster, has a living, though unmarried queen in Mistress Quickly) who die two deaths and – somewhat miraculously – both revive.

The King, too, refuses to die on the battlefield, as the crown has sent out so many doppelgangers that Douglas complains 'they grow like Hydra's heads'. For King Henry, the problem with usurping a throne is that it proves that thrones can be usurped; and it seems, in the King's mind, likely that one deposition will follow another, perhaps one even perpetrated by his son. If he can hand on the crown to Hal, a cycle of violence and civil grief can be broken – but that would only be possible if he dies and his son inherits. It's hard to break a cycle, hard to change, and it often involves a death.

Neatly underlining this is Francis' cry to the customers of the Boar's Head Tavern, 'anon, anon' – or 'soon, soon'. Falstaff is going to give up the drink, lose the weight, and return to a virtuous life. Hal is fully in control of his debauched life, using it only to prepare for his reformation. King Henry, in his first speech, lays out a plan to send troops to fight a foreign war in Jerusalem. Soon, soon; anon, anon. But not yet, not now. As characters keep saying, 'Let the end try the man.'

Robert Icke
April 2024

Player Kings was commissioned and first presented on stage by Ambassador Theatre Group Productions. It opened at the Noël Coward Theatre, London, on 11 April 2024, following previews at the New Wimbledon Theatre, London, and the Opera House, Manchester, and prior to a UK tour visiting Bristol Hippodrome, Birmingham Alexandra, Norwich Theatre Royal and Newcastle Theatre Royal. The cast was as follows (in alphabetical order):

PRINCE JOHN	Raphael Akuwudike
SNARE / DAVY	Sara Beharrell
KING HENRY IV	Richard Coyle
HOTSPUR / PISTOL	Samuel Edward-Cook
BARDOLPH	Geoffrey Freshwater
WORCESTER /	James Garnon
JUSTICE SILENCE	
MESSENGER	Alice Hayes
HARCOURT	Henry Jenkinson
PRINCE HARRY	Toheeb Jimoh
FRANCIS /	Nigel Lister
NORTHUMBERLAND	
SIR JOHN FALSTAFF	Ian McKellen
WARWICK	Annette McLaughlin
PETO	Mark Monero
SIR WALTER BLUNT	Hywel Morgan
LORD CHIEF JUSTICE	Joseph Mydell
MISTRESS QUICKLY	Clare Perkins
POINS	Daniel Rabin
SIR RICHARD VERNON	David Semark
SHERIFF	David Shelley
JUSTICE SHALLOW	Robin Soans
LADY PERCY /	Tafline Steen
DOLL TEARSHEET	
DOUGLAS / PRINCE THOMAS	Perry Williams

Adaptor & Director	Robert Icke
Set & Costume Designer	Hildegard Bechtler
Lighting Designer	Lee Curran
Sound Designer	Gareth Fry
Casting Director	Julia Horan CDG
Hair & Make-Up Designer	Susanna Peretz
Fight Director	Kev McCurdy
Associate Costume Designer	Joanna Coe
Associate Directors	Jack Bradfield
	& Lizzie Manwaring
Composer	Laura Marling
Company Stage Manager	Heidi Lennard

PRODUCERS
Ambassador Theatre Group Productions
Gavin Kalin Productions
No Guarantees Productions
David & Hannah Mirvish
Rupert Gavin & Mallory Factor Partnership
Sayers & Sayers Productions

A NOTE ON THE TEXT

The traditional act and scene divisions have been removed and replaced simply with scene numbers. And there's no punctuation other than, for clarity, the occasional forward slash (/). This is partly as we have no idea how (or if) Shakespeare would have punctuated his plays on the page; and partly to try and strip away from the play its weighty literary inheritance, the heavy sense of dusty rules, the clutter of technical terminology, and to return it simply to being sheet music for actors to act.

In the creation of *Player Kings*, various editions of *Henry IV Parts 1 & 2* have been compared, other sources have been borrowed from, words have been changed, scenes and sentences reordered, and lines reallocated. For more detail, please see the endnotes.

CHARACTERS

WESTMINSTER

KING HENRY IV *of England*
PRINCE HARRY (*or 'Hal'*), *his eldest son*
PRINCE THOMAS, *his second son*
PRINCE JOHN, *his third son*
Lady WARWICK
Sir Walter BLUNT
HARCOURT

THE LAW

The LORD CHIEF JUSTICE *of England*
SHERIFF *Fang*
Officer SNARE

NORTHUMBERLAND

Henry Percy, Earl of NORTHUMBERLAND, *a rebel lord*
Harry Percy, nicknamed 'HOTSPUR', *Northumberland's son*
Thomas Percy, Earl of WORCESTER, *Northumberland's brother*
LADY *Kate* PERCY, *Hotspur's wife*
Sir Richard VERNON, *a rebel lord*
Earl of DOUGLAS, *Scottish warlord and rebel*
MESSENGER

BOAR'S HEAD TAVERN, EASTCHEAP

MISTRESS QUICKLY, *hostess*
Sir John FALSTAFF, *knight*
BARDOLPH
PETO
Edward POINS, *nicknamed 'Ned'*
FRANCIS, *chief drawer*
SECOND DRAWER, *drawer*
DOLL TEARSHEET, *a prostitute*
PISTOL

GLOUCESTERSHIRE

Justice Robert SHALLOW, *a justice of the peace*
Justice SILENCE, *a justice of the peace*
DAVY, *head of Shallow's household*

This text went to press before the end of rehearsals and so may differ slightly from the play as performed.

ONE[1]

Westminster.

KING HENRY IV
so shaken as we are / so wan with care
find we a time for frighted peace to pant
and breathe short winded accents of new <u>wars</u>[2]
to be commenced <u>on shores</u>[3] afar remote
no more the thirsty entrance of this soil
shall daub her lips with her own children's blood
no more shall trenching war channel her fields
the edge of war like an ill-sheathed knife
no more shall cut his master / therefore friends
forthwith a power of english shall we levy
as far as to the <u>place where christ was born</u>[4]
<u>we'll make a voyage to the holy land</u>
<u>to wash the blood off from our warlike hand</u>[5]

<u>WARWICK</u>[6]
my liege / from wales <u>we have most</u>[7] heavy news
whose worst <u>is</u>[8] that young edward mortimer
<u>is by</u>[9] the men of wild glendower taken
a thousand of his people butchered
<u>and mortimer himself a prisoner</u>[10]

KING HENRY IV
it seems then that the tidings of this broil
breaks off our business for the holy land

WARWICK
<u>it will when</u>[11] matched with other / gracious lord
for more uneven and unwelcome news
comes from the north

BLUNT[12]
the gallant hotspur there
the son and heir to lord northumberland[13]
young harry percy is victorious[14]
the earl of douglas has surrendered and[15]
ten thousand scots / seven-and-twenty[16] knights
heaped[17] in their own blood did our people[18] see
on holmedon's plains / the[19] prisoners
that[20] he in this adventure hath surprised
to his own use he keeps / and sends you[21] word
you[22] shall have none

WARWICK[23]
this is his uncle's teaching / this is worcester
malevolent to you in all aspects

KING HENRY IV[24]
of prisoners hotspur took
mordake the earl of fife and eldest son
to beaten douglas / and the earls of athol
of murray / angus / and menteith
and is not this an honourable spoil?
a gallant prize? ha cousin is it not?

WARWICK[25]
in faith it is / a conquest for a prince to boast of

KING HENRY IV
yea / there thou makest me sad and makest me sin
in envy / that my lord northumberland
should be the father to so blest a son
a son who is the theme of honour's tongue
whilst i by looking on the praise of him
see riot and dishonour stain the brow
of my young harry / o that it could be proved
that some night-tripping fairy had exchanged
in cradle clothes our children where they lay
then would i have his harry and he mine

LORD CHIEF JUSTICE[26]
my liege

KING HENRY IV
but let him from my thoughts / <u>to hotspur send</u>
<u>we'll speak to him and he can</u>[27] answer this
<u>there's</u>[28] more is to be said and to be done
than out of anger can be uttered
<u>and for this cause awhile we must neglect</u>
<u>our holy purpose to jerusalem</u>[29]

TWO[30]

Boar's Head Tavern.

FALSTAFF
now hal / what time of day is it lad?

PRINCE HARRY
you are so fat-witted with drinking of old sack / and unbuttoning
yourself after supper / and sleeping on benches after noon / that
you have forgotten to demand that which you would truly know /
what the devil hast thou to do with the time of the day? unless
hours were cups of sack / and minutes chickens / and clocks
the tongues of <u>whores</u>[31] / i see no reason why you should be so
superfluous as to demand the time of the day

FALSTAFF
indeed you come near me now hal / for we that take purses go
by the moon and the seven stars / and i prithee sweet wag / when
thou art king / as god save thy grace / majesty i should say / for
grace you will have none

PRINCE HARRY
what / none?

FALSTAFF
no / not so much as will serve as prologue to an egg and butter /
marry then sweet wag / when thou art king / let us not be called
thieves / let us be gentlemen of the shade / minions of the moon

PRINCE HARRY
thou sayest well / and it holds well too / for the fortune of us that
are the moon's men ebb and flow like the sea / being governed
as the sea is by the moon / for proof / a bag of gold snatched on
monday night and spent <u>by</u>[32] tuesday morning / now in as low an
ebb as the foot of the ladder / and by and by in as high a flow as
the top of the gallows

FALSTAFF
by the lord / thou sayest true lad / and is not my hostess of the
tavern a most sweet wench?

PRINCE HARRY
is not a <u>leather jacket</u>[33] a most <u>long-wearing</u>[34] robe?

FALSTAFF
how now / how now / what have i to do with a leather jacket?

PRINCE HARRY
why / what have i to do with my hostess of the tavern?

FALSTAFF
well / you have called her to a reckoning many a time and oft

PRINCE HARRY
did i ever call for thee to pay thy part?

FALSTAFF
no i'll give thee thy due / thou hast paid all there

PRINCE HARRY
yea and elsewhere / so far as my coin would stretch / and where it
would not i have used my credit

FALSTAFF
yea / and so used it that were it not here apparent that thou art
heir apparent / but i prithee sweet wag / shall there be gallows in
england when thou art king? do not when thou art king hang a
thief

PRINCE HARRY
no / you will

FALSTAFF
shall i? o / rare / by the lord i'll be a brave judge

PRINCE HARRY
you <u>judge wrong</u>[35] already / i mean <u>you will become a hangman</u>
<u>and do the hanging of the thieves</u>[36]

FALSTAFF
well hal well / and in some sort it <u>goes</u>[37] with my humour as
well as waiting in the court / i can tell you / god's blood / i am as
melancholy as a <u>tom cat</u>[38] or a <u>baited</u>[39] bear

PRINCE HARRY
or an old lion / or a lover's lute

FALSTAFF
yea / or the drone of a lincolnshire bagpipe

PRINCE HARRY
what say you to a hare?

FALSTAFF
you have the most unsavoury <u>similes</u>[40] / and are indeed the most
comparative rascalliest sweet young prince / but hal / i prithee /
trouble me no more with vanity / i would to god you and i knew
where a supply of good names were to be bought / an old lord
of the council berated me the other day in the street about you
sir / but i marked him not / and yet he talked very wisely / but
i regarded him not / and yet he talked wisely / and in the street too

PRINCE HARRY
<u>wisdom cries out in the street and</u>[41] no man regards it

FALSTAFF
o you art able to corrupt a saint / you have done much harm
<u>upon</u>[42] me hal / god forgive you for it / before i knew you hal
i knew nothing / and now am i / if a man should speak truly /
little better than one of the wicked / i must give over this life / and
i will give it over / by the lord / if i do not i am a villain

Enter Poins.

poins / o if men were to be saved by merit / what hole in hell were hot enough for him? this is the most omnipotent villain that ever robbed[43] a true man / <u>now shall we know if they have set a match[44]</u>

PRINCE HARRY
good morrow ned

POINS
good morrow sweet hal / what says monsieur remorse? what says sir john sack and sugar? jack / how agrees the devil about your soul that you sold to him on friday last for a cup of <u>madeira-wine</u>[45] and a cold <u>chicken</u>[46] leg?

PRINCE HARRY
sir john stands to his word / he was never yet a breaker of promises / he will give the devil his due

POINS
but my lads / my lads / tomorrow morning / four o'clock / early / at gad's hill / there are traders riding to london with rich offerings and fat purses / i have <u>hoods</u>[47] for you all / you have horses for yourselves / i have bespoke supper tomorrow night in eastcheap / we may do it as secure as sleep / if you will go / i will stuff your purses full of crowns / if you will not / tarry at home and be hanged

FALSTAFF
hear ye edward / if i tarry at home and go not i'll hang you

POINS
<u>will you</u>[48] chops?

FALSTAFF
hal / will you make one?

PRINCE HARRY
who i? rob? i / a thief? not i

FALSTAFF
<u>then</u>[49] you come not of the blood royal

PRINCE HARRY
well / then once in my days i'll be a madcap

FALSTAFF
why that's well said

PRINCE HARRY
well / come what will / i'll tarry at home

FALSTAFF
by the lord / i'll be a traitor then when thou art king

PRINCE HARRY
i care not

POINS
sir john / i prithee leave the prince and me alone / i will lay him
down such reasons for this adventure that he shall come

FALSTAFF
well / god give thee[50] the spirit of persuasion / and him the ears of
profiting / farewell / you shall find me in gad's hill[51]

PRINCE HARRY
farewell thou latter spring

   Exit Falstaff.

POINS
now / my good sweet honey lord / ride with us tomorrow / i have
a jest to execute that i cannot manage alone / falstaff / bardolph
and peto shall rob those men / yourself and i shall[52] not be there /
and when they have the booty / if you and i do not rob them / cut
this head off from my shoulders

PRINCE HARRY
yea but 'tis like that they will know us by our habits and by every
other appointment to be ourselves

POINS
our masks[53] we will change after we leave them

PRINCE HARRY
yea / but i fear[54] they will be too hard for us

POINS
well / for two of them i know them to be as true-bred cowards as
ever ran away[55] and for the third / if he fight longer than he sees
reason / i'll forswear arms

PRINCE HARRY
provide us all things necessary and meet me tonight at gad's hill[56] /
farewell

POINS
farewell my lord

Exit Poins.

PRINCE HARRY
i know you all and will awhile uphold
the unyoked humour of your idleness
yet herein will i imitate the sun
who doth permit the base contagious clouds
to smother up his beauty from the world
that when he please again to be himself
being wanted he may be more wondered at
by breaking through the foul and ugly mists
of vapours that did seem to strangle him
if all the year were playing holidays
to sport would be as tedious as to work
but when they seldom come / they wished for come
so when this loose behaviour i throw off
and pay the debt i never promised
by how much better than my word i am
by so much shall i falsify men's hopes
and like bright metal on a sullen ground
my reformation glittering o'er my fault
shall show more goodly and attract more eyes
than that which hath no foil to set it off
i'll so offend / to make offence a skill
redeeming time when they[57] think least i will

THREE[58]

KING HENRY IV
my blood hath been too cold and temperate
unapt to stir at these indignities
and you have found me for accordingly
you tread upon my patience / but be sure
i will from henceforth rather be myself
mighty and to be feared

WORCESTER
our house / my sovereign liege / little deserves
the scourge of greatness to be used on it
and that same greatness too which our own hands
have <u>helped</u>[59] to make so portly

NORTHUMBERLAND
my lord

KING HENRY IV
worcester get thee gone / for i do <u>sense</u>[60]
danger and disobedience in <u>your soul</u>[61]
your presence is too bold
you have good leave to leave us / when we need
your use and counsel we shall send for you
<u>my lord northumberland</u>[62] you were about to speak

NORTHUMBERLAND
yea / my good lord
those prisoners in your highness' name demanded
which harry percy here at holmedon took
were not / he says / with such strength denied
as is <u>reported</u>[63] to your majesty
either envy therefore / or misprision
<u>is</u>[64] guilty of this fault and not my son

HOTSPUR
my liege / i did deny no prisoners
but i remember when the fight was done
when i was breathless / leaning on my sword
came there a certain lord / neat and trimly dressed

fresh as a bridegroom / and he smiled and talked
and as the soldiers bore dead bodies by
he questioned me / amongst the rest demanded
my prisoners in your majesty's behalf
i then / all smarting with my wounds being cold
out of my grief and my impatience
answered neglectingly i know not what
to see him shine so brisk and talk so sweet
of guns and drums and wounds / god save the mark
so cowardly / and but for these vile guns
he would himself have been a soldier
this bald unjointed chat of his my lord
<u>i answered</u>[65] indirectly / as i said
and i beseech you / let not <u>his</u>[66] report
come current for an accusation
betwixt my love and your high majesty

BLUNT
the circumstance considered good / my lord
whate'er <u>harry hotspur</u>[67] then had said
to such a person and in such a place
at such a time with all the rest retold
may reasonably die and never rise
to do him wrong or any way impeach
what then he said / so he unsay it now

KING HENRY IV
why yet he does deny his prisoners
but with proviso and exception
that we at our own charge shall ransom straight
his brother-in-law / the foolish mortimer
who / on my soul / hath wilfully betrayed
the lives of those that he did lead to fight
against damned glendower
whose daughter / as we hear / <u>lord mortimer</u>[68]
has lately married / shall our coffers then
be emptied to redeem a traitor home?
no / on the barren mountains let him starve
for i shall never hold that man my friend
whose tongue shall ask me for one penny cost
to ransom home revolted mortimer

NORTHUMBERLAND
my lord

HOTSPUR
revolted mortimer?
he never did revolt / my sovereign liege
but by the chance of war / to prove that true
needs no more but one tongue / for all those wounds
those mouthed wounds which valiantly he took
in single opposition with <u>your enemy</u>[69]

KING HENRY IV
thou dost belie him percy / thou dost belie him
he never did encounter <u>on our side</u>[70]
are you not ashamed? but sirrah / henceforth
let me not hear you speak of mortimer
send me your prisoners with the speediest means
or you shall hear in such a kind from me
as will displease you / my lord northumberland
we licence your departure with your son
send us your prisoners or you will hear of it

Exeunt King Henry IV, Blunt and Warwick.

HOTSPUR
<u>and</u>[71] if the devil come and roar for them
i will not send them

NORTHUMBERLAND
brother / the king hath made your nephew mad

HOTSPUR
he will forsooth have all my prisoners
and when i urged the ransom once again
<u>he trembled</u>[72] even at the name of mortimer

WORCESTER
i cannot blame him / was not he proclaimed
by richard that dead is / the next of blood?

NORTHUMBERLAND
he was

HOTSPUR
but soft / i pray you / did king richard then
proclaim my wife's brother <u>edmund</u>[73] mortimer
heir to the crown?

NORTHUMBERLAND
he did / myself did hear it

HOTSPUR
but shall it be that you that set the crown
upon the head of this forgetful man / shall it be
that you a world of curses undergo?
shall it for shame be spoken in these days
or fill up chronicles in time to come
that men of your nobility and power
did <u>pledge themselves</u>[74] in an unjust behalf
as both of you / god pardon it / have done?
<u>and are you</u>[75] fooled / discarded and shook off
by him for whom these shames ye underwent?
no / yet time serves wherein you may redeem
your banished honours and restore yourselves
into the good thoughts of the world again
revenge the jeering and disdained contempt
of this proud king

WORCESTER
                              peace cousin / say no more
and now i will unclasp a secret book
<u>and</u>[76] read you matter deep and dangerous

HOTSPUR
send danger from the east unto the west
so honour cross it from the north to south

NORTHUMBERLAND
imagination of some great exploit
drives him beyond the bounds of patience

HOTSPUR
by heaven / methinks it were an easy leap
to pluck bright honour from the pale-faced moon
or dive into the bottom of the deep

WORCESTER
good cousin / give me audience for a while

HOTSPUR
i cry you mercy

WORCESTER
               those same noble scots
that are your prisoners

HOTSPUR
               i'll keep them all
by god he shall not have a scot of them
no / if a scot would save his soul he shall not
i'll keep them by this hand

WORCESTER
             you start away
and lend no ear unto my purposes
those prisoners you shall keep

HOTSPUR
             nay i will / that's flat
all studies here i solemnly defy
save how to gall and pinch this bolingbroke
and that same sword-and-buckler prince of wales
but that i think his father loves him not
and would be glad he met with some mischance
i'd have him poisoned with a pot of ale

WORCESTER
farewell kinsman / i'll talk to you
when you are better tempered to attend

NORTHUMBERLAND
why what a <u>wasp-stung</u>[77] and impatient fool

HOTSPUR
good uncle tell your tale / i have done

WORCESTER
nay if you have not / to it again
we will stay your leisure

HOTSPUR
                    i have done i'faith[78]

WORCESTER
then once more to your scottish prisoners
release them / now / without a ransom straight
and make lord douglas then[79] your only man[80]
for raising[81] powers in scotland
i speak not this in estimation
as what i think might be / but what i know
is ruminated / plotted and set down
and only stays but to behold the face
of that occasion that shall bring it on

HOTSPUR
why / it cannot choose but be a noble plot
and then the power of scotland and the north[82]
to join with mortimer?

WORCESTER
                    and so they shall

HOTSPUR
in faith / it is exceedingly well aimed

WORCESTER
and 'tis no little reason bids us speed
for bear ourselves as even as we can
the king will always think him in our debt
and think we are ourselves unsatisfied
till he hath found a time to pay us home
and see already how he doth begin
to make us strangers to his looks of love

HOTSPUR
he does / he does / we'll be revenged on him

WORCESTER
i'll to glendower and lord mortimer
where you and douglas and our powers at once
as i will fashion it / shall happily meet

NORTHUMBERLAND
farewell good brother / we shall thrive i trust?

HOTSPUR
uncle adieu / o let the hours be short
till fields / and blows / and groans applaud our sport

FOUR[83]

Gad's Hill.

POINS
come / shelter / shelter / <u>there's a gentleman[84] hath brought three hundred marks with him in gold / they heard him tell it to one of his company last night at supper / they are up already and call for eggs and butter</u>[85] / they will away at once

FALSTAFF (*off*)
<u>poins</u>[86]

POINS
and i have removed falstaff's horse / and he frets like a <u>turkey at christmas</u>[87]

FALSTAFF (*off*)
<u>poins</u>[88]

PRINCE HARRY
stand close

   Enter Falstaff.

FALSTAFF
poins / poins and be hanged / poins

PRINCE HARRY
peace ye fat-kidneyed <u>bastard</u>[89] / what a brawling dost thou keep

FALSTAFF
where's poins / hal?

PRINCE HARRY

he is walked up to the top of the hill / i'll go seek him

FALSTAFF

i am accursed to rob in that thief's company / the rascal hath
removed my horse and tied him i know not where / if i travel
but four foot further i shall <u>lose</u>[90] my wind / well i doubt not but
to die a fair death for all this / if i 'scape hanging for killing that
rogue <u>poins</u>[91] / i have forsworn his company hourly any time this
two-and-twenty years / and yet i am bewitched with the rogue's
company / if the rascal have not given me medicines to make me
love him i'll be hanged / poins / hal / a plague upon you both /
bardolph / peto / i'll starve ere i'll rob a foot further / <u>if it</u>[92] were
not <u>a good deed</u>[93] to turn true man and to leave these rogues /
i am the veriest varlet that ever chewed with a tooth / a plague
upon it when thieves cannot be true one to another / a plague
upon you all / give me my horse you rogue / give me my horse and
be hanged

PRINCE HARRY

peace ye fat guts / lie down close to the ground and list if thou
canst hear the tread of travellers

FALSTAFF

have you any levers to lift me up again being down? god's blood /
i'll not bear mine own flesh so far afoot again for all the coin in
your father's exchequer / i prithee / good prince hal / help me to
my horse

PRINCE HARRY

out ye rogue / <u>am i your stable boy?</u>[94]

FALSTAFF

<u>go</u>[95] hang thyself in your own heir-apparent garters / if i be taken /
i'll <u>change sides</u>[96] for this

Enter Peto and Bardolph.

<u>PETO</u>[97]

stand

FALSTAFF
so i do / against my will

POINS
o 'tis our setter / i know his voice / <u>peto</u>[98] / <u>what news?</u>[99]

<u>PETO</u>[100]
on with your <u>masks</u>[101] / there's money of the king's coming down
the hill / 'tis going to the king's exchequer

PRINCE HARRY
sirs / you <u>three</u>[102] shall front them here in the narrow lane / ned
poins and i will walk lower / if they 'scape from your encounter
then they light on us

<u>BARDOLPH</u>[103]
how many be <u>there</u>[104] of them?

<u>PETO</u>[105]
some eight or ten

FALSTAFF
will they not rob us?

PRINCE HARRY
what a coward / sir john paunch?

FALSTAFF
i am not john of gaunt your grandfather / but yet no coward hal

PRINCE HARRY
well / we leave that to the proof

FALSTAFF
come my masters / every man to his business

POINS
jack / your horse stands behind the hedge / when you need him /
there <u>you'll</u>[106] find him

FALSTAFF
now cannot i strike him

PRINCE HARRY
ned / where are our disguises?

POINS
here / stand close

Enter Travellers.

FALSTAFF
strike / down with them / cut the villains' throats / ah / whoreson
caterpillars / bacon-fed knaves / you <u>potbellied</u>[107] knaves / are ye
undone? no / ye fat <u>misers</u>[108] / young men must live

Falstaff, Peto and Bardolph rob the Travellers.

FALSTAFF
come my masters / let us share and then to <u>london</u>[109] before day / <u>if</u>[110]
the prince and poins be not two arrant cowards / there's no equity
stirring / there's no more valour in that poins than in a wild duck

Enter Prince Harry and Poins.

PRINCE HARRY
your money

Bardolph, Falstaff and Peto run away.

PRINCE HARRY
got with much ease / now merrily to horse
the thieves are all scattered and possessed with fear
falstaff <u>sweats</u>[111] to death
and lards the lean earth as he walks along
were't not for laughing / i should pity him

POINS
how the rogue roared

FIVE[112]

Westminster.

KING HENRY IV
how many thousand of my poorest subjects
are at this hour asleep / o sleep / o gentle sleep
nature's soft nurse / how have i frighted thee
that thou no more wilt weigh my eyelids down
and steep my senses in forgetfulness?
why rather / sleep / liest thou in smoky cribs
and hushed with buzzing night flies to thy slumber
than in the perfumed chambers of the great
under the canopies of costly state
and lulled with sound of sweetest melody?
o thou dull god / why liest thou with the vile
in loathsome beds and leavest the kingly couch
a watch-case or a common 'larum-bell?
wilt thou / upon the high and giddy mast
seal up the ship-boy's eyes and rock his brains
in cradle of the rude imperious surge
and in the visitation of the winds
who take the ruffian <u>billows</u>[113] by the top
curling their monstrous heads and hanging them
with <u>deafening</u>[114] clamour in the slippery clouds
that with the hurly death itself awakes?
canst thou / o partial sleep / give thy repose
to the wet sea-boy in an hour so rude
and in the calmest and most stillest night
with all appliances and means to boot
deny it to a king? then happy low lie down
uneasy lies the head that wears a crown

SIX[115]

Boar's Head Tavern.

PRINCE HARRY
when i am king of england i shall command all the good lads in
eastcheap[116] / sirrah / i am sworn brother to a leash of servants[117]
and can call them all by their christian[118] names / though i be but
the prince of wales yet / i am king of courtesy / and they tell me
flatly / i am a lad of mettle / a good boy by the lord / so they call
me / i tell thee ned / thou hast lost much honour that thou wert
not with me in this action

but sweet ned / to sweeten which name i give thee this
pennyworth of sugar / clapped even now into my hand by an
under-skinker / one that never spake other english in his life than
'anon anon sir'

POINS
francis?

PRINCE HARRY
thou art perfect

POINS (*calls*)
francis

   Enter Francis.

FRANCIS
anon anon sir

PRINCE HARRY
come hither francis

FRANCIS
my lord?

PRINCE HARRY
how old art thou francis?

FRANCIS
let me see / about michaelmas next i shall be

POINS
francis

FRANCIS
anon anon sir / pray stay a little my lord

PRINCE HARRY
nay / but hark you francis / for the sugar thou gavest

POINS
<u>francis</u>

FRANCIS
<u>anon sir</u>[119]

PRINCE HARRY
i will give thee for it a thousand pound / ask me when thou wilt
and thou shalt have it

POINS
francis

FRANCIS
anon anon

PRINCE HARRY
anon francis? no francis / but tomorrow francis? or francis on
thursday / or indeed francis when thou wilt

POINS
<u>francis</u>

FRANCIS
<u>anon</u>[120]

PRINCE HARRY
but francis

FRANCIS
my lord?

PRINCE HARRY
wilt thou rob this leathern jerkin / crystal-button / knot-pated /
agate-ring / puke-stocking caddis-garter / smooth-tongue /
spanish-pouch?

FRANCIS
o lord sir / who do you mean?

POINS
francis

PRINCE HARRY
francis

MISTRESS QUICKLY[121]
what / do you stand still at[122] such a calling? look to the guests
within / my lord / old sir john with half-a-dozen more are at the
door / shall i let them in?

PRINCE HARRY
let them alone awhile / and then open the door

Exit Mistress Quickly.

PRINCE HARRY
i am now of all humours that have showed themselves humours
since the old days of adam to this present twelve o'clock at
midnight / i am not yet of percy's mind / the hotspur of the
north / he that kills me some six or seven dozen of scots at a
breakfast / washes his hands / and says to his wife 'fie upon
this quiet life / i want work' / 'o my sweet harry' says she 'how
many hast thou killed today?' and he[123] answers / i prithee call in
falstaff / i'll play percy and that damned brawn shall play dame
mortimer his wife / call in ribs

Enter Mistress Quickly with Falstaff, Bardolph and Peto.

POINS
welcome jack / where have you been?

FALSTAFF
a plague on all cowards i say / and a vengeance too / marry and

amen / give me a cup of sack boy / a plague on[124] all cowards / give me a cup of sack rogue / is there no virtue left[125]

Francis hands Falstaff a cup of sack.

rogue / there's lime in this / there is nothing but roguery to be found in villainous man / yet a coward is worse / a villanous coward / go thy ways old jack / die when thou wilt / if manhood good manhood be not forgot upon the face of the earth then i am[126] a shotten herring / there live not three good men unhanged in england / and one of them is fat and grows old / god help the while / a bad world / a plague of all cowards i say still

PRINCE HARRY
how now wool-sack / what mutter you?

FALSTAFF
a king's son / if i do not beat you out of your kingdom with a wooden dagger[127] and drive all your subjects before you like a flock of wild-geese / i'll never wear hair on my face more / you? prince of wales?

PRINCE HARRY
why you whoreson round man / what's the matter?

FALSTAFF
are you not[128] a coward? answer me to that / and poins there

POINS
zounds ye fat paunch / you call me coward / by the lord / i'll stab you

FALSTAFF
i call thee coward / i'll see thee damned ere i call thee coward / but i would give a thousand pound to[129] run as fast as you can / you care not who sees your back / call you that backing of your friends? a plague upon such backing / give me them that will face me / give me a cup of sack / i am a rogue if i drunk today

PRINCE HARRY
o villain / thy lips are scarce wiped since you drank last

FALSTAFF
all's one for that / a plague on all cowards still say i

PRINCE HARRY
what's the matter?

FALSTAFF
what's the matter? there be <u>three</u>[130] of us here have taken a
thousand pound this morning

PRINCE HARRY
where is it jack? where is it?

FALSTAFF
where is it? taken from us it is / a hundred <u>of them</u>[131] on <u>us</u>[132] poor
<u>three</u>[133]

PRINCE HARRY
what? a hundred men?

FALSTAFF
i am a rogue if i were not at half-sword with a dozen of them two
hours together / i have escaped by miracle / i am eight times thrust
through the <u>shirt</u>[134] / my <u>blade</u>[135] hacked like a handsaw / <u>behold
the proof</u>[136] / i never <u>fought</u>[137] better since i was a man / all would
not do / a plague of all cowards / let them speak / if they speak
more or less than truth they are villains and the sons of darkness

PRINCE HARRY
speak sirs / how was it?

BARDOLPH
we <u>three</u>[138] set upon some dozen

FALSTAFF
sixteen at least my lord

BARDOLPH
and bound them

PETO
no / no they were not bound

FALSTAFF
you rogue / <u>we bound them</u>[139] / every man of them

BARDOLPH
as we were sharing / some six or seven fresh men set upon us

FALSTAFF
and unbound the rest / and then come in the others

PRINCE HARRY
what fought you with them all?

FALSTAFF
all / i know not what you call all / but if i fought not with fifty
of them / i am a bunch of radish / if there were not two and fifty
or three and fifty upon poor old jack / then am i no two-legged
creature

<u>PRINCE HARRY</u>[140]
pray god you have not murdered some of them

FALSTAFF
nay that's past praying for / i have peppered two of them / two
i am sure i have paid / two rogues in buckram suits / i tell thee
what hal / if i tell you a lie / spit in my face / call me horse / you
know my old <u>defence</u>[141] / here i lay / and thus i bore my point /
four rogues in buckram suits let drive at me

PRINCE HARRY
what / four? you said but two even now

FALSTAFF
four hal / i told thee four

POINS
ay / ay / he said four

FALSTAFF
these four came all a-front / and mainly thrust at me / i made me
no more ado but took all their seven points in my target thus

PRINCE HARRY
seven? why / there were but four even now

FALSTAFF
in buckram?

POINS
ay / four in buckram suits

FALSTAFF
seven by this sword[142] / or i am a villain else

PRINCE HARRY
prithee let him alone / we shall have more anon

FALSTAFF
do you hear me hal?

PRINCE HARRY
ay / and mark thee too jack

FALSTAFF
do so / for it is worth the listening to / these nine in buckram that
i told you of

PRINCE HARRY
so two more already

FALSTAFF
began to give me ground / but i followed me close / came in foot
and hand / and with a thought / seven of the eleven i paid

PRINCE HARRY
o monstrous / eleven buckram men grown out of two

FALSTAFF
but as the devil would have it / three misbegotten knaves all
wearing[143] green came at my back and let drive at me / for it was
so dark hal that you could not see your hand

PRINCE HARRY
these lies are like their father that begets them / gross as a
mountain / open / palpable / why you clay-brained guts / thou
knotty-pated fool / thou whoreson obscene greasy tallow-catch

FALSTAFF
what / are you mad? are you mad? is not the truth the truth?

PRINCE HARRY
why / how could you know these men <u>were all wearing</u>[144] green /
when it was so dark you could not see your hand? come / tell us
your reason / what say you to this?

POINS
come / your reason jack / your reason

FALSTAFF
what / upon compulsion? / <u>if i were tortured on all the racks</u>[145] in
the world i would not tell you on compulsion / give you a reason
on compulsion / if reasons were as plentiful as blackberries i would
give no man a reason upon compulsion

PRINCE HARRY
i'll be no longer guilty of this sin / this sanguine coward / this bed-
presser / this horseback-breaker / this huge hill of flesh

FALSTAFF
you starveling / you <u>elf-skin</u>[146] / you dried cow's tongue / you bull's
pizzle / o for breath to utter what is like thee / you sheath / you
bow-case / you vile standing-tuck

PRINCE HARRY
well / breathe a while / and then to it again / and when you have
<u>tired</u>[147] yourself in base comparisons hear me speak but this

POINS
mark jack

PRINCE HARRY
we two saw you <u>three</u>[148] set on four / and bound them / and were
masters of their wealth / mark now how a plain tale shall put you
down / then did we two set on you <u>three</u>[149]/ and with a <u>shout</u>[150]
out-faced you from your prize / and have it / yea / and can show it
you / here in the house

and falstaff / you carried your guts away as nimbly / with as quick
dexterity / and roared for mercy / and still run and roared as ever

i heard a <u>baby cow</u>[151] / what a slave art thou to hack thy sword
as thou hast done and then say it was in fight? what trick / what
device / what starting-hole can you now find out to hide you from
this open and apparent shame?

POINS
come / let's hear jack

FALSTAFF
by the lord i knew you as well as he that made you / why hear you
my masters / was it for me to kill the heir apparent? should i turn
upon the true prince? why / you know i am as valiant as hercules /
but beware instinct / the lion will not touch the true prince /
instinct is a great matter / i was now a coward on instinct / i shall
think the better of myself and you during my life / i for a valiant
lion and you for a true prince / but by the lord lads / i am glad you
have the money

hostess / clap to the doors / watch tonight / pray tomorrow /
gallants / lads / boys / hearts of gold / shall we be merry? shall we
have a play?

PRINCE HARRY
content and the argument shall be you running away

FALSTAFF
ah / no more of that hal / if you love me

MISTRESS QUICKLY
o jesu / my lord the prince / there is a nobleman of the court at
door would speak with you / he says he comes from your father

FALSTAFF
what manner of man is he?

MISTRESS QUICKLY
an old man

FALSTAFF
what doth gravity out of his bed at midnight? shall i give him his
answer?

PRINCE HARRY
prithee do jack

FALSTAFF
'faith / i'll send him packing

   Exit Falstaff.

PRINCE HARRY
now / by our lady / bardolph / you fought fair / so did you peto /
you are lions too / you ran away upon instinct / you will not touch
the true prince

BARDOLPH
'faith / i ran when i saw others run

PRINCE HARRY
'faith / now tell me in earnest / how came falstaff's sword so
hacked?

PETO
why / he hacked it with his dagger / and said he would swear truth
out of england but he would make you believe it was done in fight

BARDOLPH
yea and to beslubber our garments with <u>raw steak</u>[152] and swear it
the blood of true men

   Re-enter Falstaff.

PRINCE HARRY
here comes lean jack / here comes bare-bone / how now my sweet
creature of bombast / how long is it ago jack since you saw your
own knee?

FALSTAFF
my own knee / when i was about your years hal / i was not an
eagle's talon in the waist / i could have crept into any alderman's
thumb-ring / a plague of sighing and grief / it blows a man up like
a bladder

there's villainous news abroad / you must to the court in the morning / that same mad fellow of the north / what a plague call you him?

POINS
hotspur[153]

FALSTAFF
harry hotspur[154] / the same / and old northumberland / and that sprightly scot of scots douglas / that runs on horseback[155] up a hill perpendicular / well he is there too

worcester is gone to their side[156] tonight[157] / thy father's hair[158] is turned white with the news / you may buy land now as cheap as stinking mackerel / but[159] by the mass lad / art not thou horrible afeard? / thou being heir-apparent / could the world pick thee out three such enemies again as douglas / glendower / and hotspur?[160] art thou not horribly afraid?

PRINCE HARRY
not a whit / i lack some of thy instinct

FALSTAFF
well / you will be horribly chid tomorrow when you come to your father / if you love me / practise an answer

PRINCE HARRY
you stand for my father / and examine me upon the particulars of my life

FALSTAFF
shall i? content / this chair shall be my state / this dagger my sceptre / and this cushion my crown / if the fire of grace be not quite out of thee / now shalt thou be moved / give me a cup of sack / to make my eyes look red / that it may be thought i have wept / for i must speak in passion / stand aside nobility

MISTRESS QUICKLY
o jesu / this is excellent sport in faith

FALSTAFF
weep not / sweet queen / for trickling tears are vain

MISTRESS QUICKLY
o the father / how he holds his countenance

FALSTAFF
for god's sake / lords convey my tristful queen

MISTRESS QUICKLY
o jesu / he doth it as like one of these players as ever i see

FALSTAFF
peace good pint-pot / peace good tickle-brain

harry / i do not only marvel where thou spendest thy time / but
also how thou art accompanied / for though the camomile / the
more it is trodden on / the faster it grows / yet[161] youth / the more
it is wasted / the sooner it wears

that thou art my son / i have partly thy mother's word / partly my
own opinion / if then thou be son to me / here lies the point /
why being son to me art thou so pointed at? shall the son of
england prove a thief and take purses? a question to be asked / for
harry / now i do not speak to thee in drink / but in tears / not in
pleasure / but in passion / not in words only / but in woes also /
and yet there is a virtuous man whom i have often noted in thy
company / but i know not his name

PRINCE HARRY
what manner of man an it like your majesty?

FALSTAFF
a goodly portly man i'faith / and a corpulent / of a cheerful
look / a pleasing eye and a most noble carriage / and as i think
his age some fifty / or by 'r lady inclining to threescore / and now
i remember me his name is falstaff / if that man should be lewdly
given he deceiveth me / for harry i see virtue in his looks / there
is virtue in that falstaff / him keep with / the rest banish / and tell
me now thou naughty varlet / tell me where hast thou been this
month?

PRINCE HARRY
do you speak like a king? you stand for me and i'll play my father

FALSTAFF
depose me? if thou dost it half so majestically / both in word and matter / hang me up by the heels for a rabbit-sucker

PRINCE HARRY
well / here i am set

FALSTAFF
here i stand / judge my masters

PRINCE HARRY
now harry / whence come you?

FALSTAFF
my noble lord / from eastcheap

PRINCE HARRY
the complaints i hear of thee are grievous

FALSTAFF
god's blood / my lord / they are false

PRINCE HARRY
swearest thou ungracious boy? from henceforth never look on me again[162] / thou art violently carried away from grace / there is a devil haunts thee in the likeness of an old fat man / a tonne[163] of man is thy companion / why dost thou converse with that trunk of humours / that bolting-hutch of beastliness / that swollen parcel of dropsies / that huge bombard of sack / that stuffed cloak-bag of guts / that roasted manningtree ox with the pudding in his belly / that reverend vice / that grey iniquity / that father ruffian / that vanity in years / wherein is he good but to taste sack and drink it? but to carve a chicken[164] and eat it? wherein cunning but in craft? wherein crafty but in villainy? wherein villainous but in everything? wherein worthy but in nothing?

FALSTAFF
i would your grace would take me with you / whom means your grace?

PRINCE HARRY
that villainous / abominable / misleader of youth / falstaff / that
old white-bearded satan

FALSTAFF
my lord / the man i know

PRINCE HARRY
i know thou dost

FALSTAFF
but to say i know more harm in him than in myself were to say
more than i know / that he is old / the more the pity / his white
hairs do witness it / but that he is / saving your reverence / a
whoremaster / that i utterly deny / if sack and sugar be a fault
god[165] help the wicked / if to be old and merry be a sin then many
an old host that i know is damned / if to be fat is to be hated then
pharaoh's lean kine are to be loved / no my good lord / banish
peto / banish bardolph / banish poins / but for sweet jack falstaff /
kind jack falstaff / true jack falstaff / valiant jack falstaff / and
therefore more valiant / being as he is old jack falstaff / banish not
him thy harry's company / banish not him thy harry's company /
banish plump jack and banish all the world

PRINCE HARRY
i do / i will

MISTRESS QUICKLY
the sheriff and all the watch are at the door / they are come to
search the house

FALSTAFF
out ye rogue / play out the play / i have much to say on[166] behalf
of that falstaff[167]

MISTRESS QUICKLY
o jesu / my lord / my lord

PRINCE HARRY
hey hey / what's the matter?

BARDOLPH
o my lord / my lord / the sheriff with a most monstrous watch is at the door[168]

FALSTAFF[169]
do you hear hal? never call a true piece of gold a counterfeit

PRINCE HARRY
hide thee behind the arras / the rest walk up above / now my masters / for a true face and good conscience

> *Enter Sheriff, the Carrier, Lord Chief Justice[170] and other officers.[171]*

PRINCE HARRY
now master sheriff / what is your will with me?

LORD CHIEF JUSTICE
i pray you / your grace / know you who i am?

PRINCE HARRY
you / who knows not you?
why man / you are lord chief justice of england

LORD CHIEF JUSTICE
i am glad to see your grace in good health
a hue and cry hath followed certain men unto this house[172]

PRINCE HARRY
what men?

SHERIFF
one of them is well known / my gracious lord / a gross fat man

CARRIER
as fat as butter

PRINCE HARRY
the man i do assure you is not here
for i myself at this time have employed him
and sheriff / i will engage my word to thee
that i will by tomorrow dinner time
send him to answer thee / or any man

for anything he shall be charged withal
and so let me entreat you leave the house

SHERIFF
i will / my lord

LORD CHIEF JUSTICE[173]
there are two gentlemen have in this robbery lost three hundred
marks

PRINCE HARRY
it may be so / if he have robbed these men
he shall be answerable

Enter Bardolph restrained by the officers.

CARRIER
that's the other[174]

PRINCE HARRY
my lord / this is my man[175]

LORD CHIEF JUSTICE
you'll find small credit to acknowledge him

PRINCE HARRY
but what mean you to do with him?

LORD CHIEF JUSTICE
so please your grace / the law must pass on him

PRINCE HARRY
why / then belike you mean to hang my man?

LORD CHIEF JUSTICE
i am sorry that it falls out so

PRINCE HARRY
why / my lord / know you who i am?

LORD CHIEF JUSTICE
and please your grace / you are my lord the young prince / our

king that shall be after the decease of the sovereign king henry the fourth / whom god grant long to reign

PRINCE HARRY
and you will hang my man?

LORD CHIEF JUSTICE
so please your grace / i must needs do justice

PRINCE HARRY
tell me my lord / shall i have my man?

LORD CHIEF JUSTICE
i cannot my lord

PRINCE HARRY
will you not let him go?

LORD CHIEF JUSTICE
i cannot / nor i may not

PRINCE HARRY
no / then i will have him

Prince Harry gives Lord Chief Justice a box on the ear.

POINS
my lord / shall i cut off his head

PRINCE HARRY
no / i charge you draw not your swords / but get you hence

LORD CHIEF JUSTICE
in striking me in this place you greatly abuse me / and also your father / whose person in this place i represent

Exeunt Lord Chief Justice and Carrier.

SHERIFF
good night my noble lord

PRINCE HARRY
i think it is good morrow / is it not?

SHERIFF
indeed my lord / i think it be two o'clock

Exit Sheriff.

PRINCE HARRY
this oily <u>bastard</u>[176] is known as well as <u>st.</u>[177] paul's / go call him
forth

PETO
falstaff / fast asleep behind the arras / snorting like a horse

PRINCE HARRY
hark how hard he fetches breath / search his pockets

Peto searches Falstaff's pockets.

what hast thou found?

PETO
nothing but papers my lord

PRINCE HARRY
let's see what <u>they be</u>[178] / read them

PETO
item / a <u>chicken</u>[179] / 2s 2d
item / sauce / 4d
item / sack / two gallons / 5s 8d
item / anchovies and sack after supper / 2s 6d
item / bread / <u>halfpence</u>[180]

PRINCE HARRY
o monstrous / one half-pennyworth of bread to this intolerable
deal of sack / what there is else keep close / we'll read it at more
advantage / there let him sleep till day / i'll to the court in the
morning and thy place shall be honourable / the money shall
be paid back again with advantage / be with me betimes in the
morning / and so good morrow peto

PETO
good morrow / good my lord

SEVEN[181]

Westminster.

KING HENRY IV
lords give us leave / the prince of wales and i
must have some private conference / but be near at hand

Exeunt Warwick and Lord Chief Justice.

i know not whether god[182] will have it so
for some displeasing service i have done
that in his secret doom out of my blood
he'll breed revengement and a scourge for me
but thou dost in thy[183] passages of life
make me believe that thou art only made[184]
to punish my mistreadings / tell me how else
could such inordinate and low desires
such poor / such bare / such lewd / such mean attempts
such barren pleasures / rude society
as thou art matched withal and grafted to
accompany the greatness of thy blood
and hold their level with thy princely heart?

PRINCE HARRY
so please your majesty / i would i could
quit all offences with as clear excuse
as well as i am doubtless i can purge
myself of many i am charged withal
yet such extenuation let me beg
as in reproof of many tales devised
by smiling pickthanks and base newsmongers
i may for some things true / wherein my youth
hath faulty wandered and irregular
find pardon on my true submission

KING HENRY IV
god pardon thee
yet let me wonder harry at thy affections
thy place in council thou hast rudely lost

which by thy younger brother is supplied
and art almost an alien to the hearts
of all the court and princes of my blood
the hope and expectation of thy time
is ruined and the soul of every man
prophetically doth forethink thy fall
had i so lavish of my presence been
so common-hackneyed in the eyes of men
so stale and cheap to vulgar company
opinion / that did help me to the crown
had left me in reputeless banishment
a fellow of no mark nor likelihood
i dressed myself in such humility
that i did pluck allegiance from men's hearts
the skipping king / he ambled up and down
grew a companion to the common streets
and in that very line harry standest thou
for thou has lost thy princely privilege
with vile participation / not an eye
but is aweary of thy common sight
save mine which hath desired to see thee more
which now doth that i would not have it do
make blind itself with foolish tenderness

PRINCE HARRY
i shall hereafter / my thrice gracious lord
be more myself

KING HENRY IV
                     for all the world
as thou art to this hour / was richard then
now / by my sceptre and my soul to boot
young hotspur[185] has more interest to the state
than thou / the shadow of succession
what never-dying honour hath he got
thrice hath this hotspur / mars in swathling[186] clothes
this infant warrior in his enterprises
discomfited great douglas / and hath won
and what say you to this? hotspur[187] / northumberland
lord worcester[188]/ douglas / mortimer
capitulate against us and in arms[189]

but wherefore do i tell these news to you?
why / harry / do i tell you of my foes
which art my near'st and dearest enemy?
thou that art like enough / through simple fear
to fight against me under percy's pay

PRINCE HARRY
do not think so / you shall not find it so
and god[190] forgive them that so much have swayed
your majesty's good thoughts away from me
i will redeem all this on hotspur's[191] head
and in the closing of some glorious day
be bold to tell you that i am your son
when i will wear a garment all of blood
and stain my favours in a bloody mask
which washed away shall scour my shame with it
if not / the end of life cancels all bands
and i will die a hundred thousand deaths
ere break the smallest parcel of this vow

KING HENRY IV
a hundred thousand rebels die in this

Enter Blunt.

how now good blunt? thy looks are full of speed

BLUNT
so is[192] the business that i come to speak of
a mighty and a fearful force they are

KING HENRY IV
our hands are full of business / let's away
advantage feeds him fat while men delay

EIGHT[193]

Boar's Head Tavern.

FALSTAFF
bardolph / am i not fallen away vilely since this last action on gad's
hill? do i not bate? do i not dwindle? why / my skin hangs about
me like an old lady's loose gown / i am withered like an old apple /
well / i'll repent while i am in some liking / if i have not forgotten
what the inside of a church is made of i am a peppercorn / the
inside of a church / company / villainous company hath been the
spoil of me

BARDOLPH
sir john / you are so fretful / you cannot live long

FALSTAFF
why / there is it / come / sing me a bawdy song / make me merry /
i was as virtuously given as a gentleman need to be / virtuous
enough / swore little / gambled[194] not / above seven times / a
week / went to a whore-house[195] once / in a quarter / of an hour /
paid money that i borrowed three or four times / lived well and in
good compass / and now i live out of all order / out of all compass

BARDOLPH
why / you are so fat sir john that you must needs be out of all
compass / out of all reasonable compass sir john

FALSTAFF
amend thy face and i'll amend my life

   Enter Mistress Quickly.

have you inquired yet who picked my pocket?

MISTRESS QUICKLY
why sir john / what do you think sir john? do you think i keep
thieves in my house? i have searched / i have inquired / man by
man / boy by boy / servant by servant / so much as[196] a hair was
never lost in my house before

FALSTAFF
you lie hostess / my pocket was picked / go to / i know you well
enough

MISTRESS QUICKLY
no sir john / you do not know me sir john / i know you sir john /
you owe me money sir john / and now you pick a quarrel to
beguile me of it / i bought you a dozen of shirts to your back

FALSTAFF
shirts / filthy shirts[197] / i have given them away

MISTRESS QUICKLY
now as i am a true woman / you owe money here besides sir john /
for your diet and by-drinkings / and money lent you / four-and-
twenty pound[198]

FALSTAFF
he had his part of it / let him pay

MISTRESS QUICKLY
he? alas he is poor / he hath nothing

FALSTAFF
how / poor? look upon his face / what call you rich? let them coin
his nose / i'll not pay a farthing[199] / shall i not take my ease in my
inn but i shall have my pocket picked? i have lost a seal-ring of my
grandfather's worth forty mark

MISTRESS QUICKLY
i have heard the prince tell him i know not how oft that ring was
copper

FALSTAFF
how / the prince is a jack / a sneak / and were he here[200] i would
cudgel him like a dog if he would say so

   Enter Prince Harry in military fatigues.[201]

how now lad / is the wind in that door? must we all march?

MISTRESS QUICKLY
my lord / i pray you / hear me

PRINCE HARRY
what say'st thou mistress quickly?

FALSTAFF
prithee let her alone and list to me

PRINCE HARRY
what say'st thou jack?

FALSTAFF
the other night i fell asleep here behind the arras and had my
pocket picked

PRINCE HARRY
what didst thou lose jack?

FALSTAFF
wilt thou believe me hal? three or four bonds of forty pound
apiece / and a seal-ring of my grandfather's

PRINCE HARRY
a trifle / some eight-penny matter

MISTRESS QUICKLY
so i told him my lord / and i said i heard your grace say so / and
my lord he speaks most vilely of you / like a foul-mouthed man as
he is and said he would cudgel you

PRINCE HARRY
what? he did not

MISTRESS QUICKLY
and said the other day you owed him a thousand pound

PRINCE HARRY
sirrah / do i owe you a thousand pound?

FALSTAFF
a thousand pound hal? a million / thy love is worth a million /
thou owest me thy love

MISTRESS QUICKLY
nay my lord / he called you jack / and he said he would cudgel you

FALSTAFF
did i bardolph?

BARDOLPH
indeed / sir john / you said so

FALSTAFF
yea / if he said my ring was copper

PRINCE HARRY
i say 'tis copper / darest thou be as good as thy word now?

FALSTAFF
why / hal as thou art but man i dare / but as thou art prince /
i fear thee as i fear the roaring of a lion cub

PRINCE HARRY
and why not as the lion?

FALSTAFF
the king is to be feared as the lion / do you think i'll fear you? as
i fear thy father? nay if i do / <u>pray god</u>[202] my girdle break

PRINCE HARRY
if it should how would thy guts fall about thy knees / charge an
honest woman with picking thy pocket / if there were anything
in thy pocket but tavern-reckonings / memorandums of bawdy-
houses and one poor penny-worth of sugar-candy / if thy pocket
were enriched with any other injuries but these / i am a villain /
are you not ashamed?

FALSTAFF
you see / i have more flesh than other man / and therefore more
frailty / you confess then / you picked my pocket?

PRINCE HARRY
it appears so / by the story

FALSTAFF
hostess / i forgive thee / go make ready breakfast / look to thy
servants / cherish thy guests / thou shalt find me tractable to any
honest reason / thou seest i am pacified still / nay prithee be gone

Exit Mistress Quickly.

now hal / to the news at court / for the robbery lad / how is that
answered?

PRINCE HARRY
the money is paid back again

FALSTAFF
o / i do not like that paying back / 'tis a double labour

PRINCE HARRY
i am good friends with my father and may do anything

FALSTAFF
rob me the exchequer the first thing thou dost

BARDOLPH
do my lord

PRINCE HARRY
i have procured thee jack a regiment[203]
meet me tomorrow in the temple hall
at two o'clock in the afternoon
there shalt thou have thy charge and there receive
money and order for their furnishing[204]
the land is burning / hotspur[205] stands on high
and either we or they[206] must lower lie

Exit Prince Harry.

FALSTAFF
rare words / brave world / hostess my breakfast come
o / i could wish this tavern were my drum

NINE[207]

Northumberland.

LADY PERCY
o my good lord / why are you thus alone?
for what offence have i this fortnight been
a banished woman from my harry's bed?
tell me / sweet lord / what is't that takes from thee
thy stomach pleasure and thy golden sleep?
why dost thou bend thine eyes upon the earth
and start so often when thou sit'st alone?
why has thou lost the fresh blood in thy cheeks
and given my treasures and my rights of thee
to thick-eyed musing and curst melancholy?
why comes your father here / and mortimer?[208]
thy spirit within thee hath been so at war
and thus hath so bestirred thee in thy sleep
that beads[209] of sweat have stood upon thy brow
like bubbles in a late-disturbed stream
and in thy face strange motions have appeared
such as we see when men restrain their breath
some heavy business hath my lord in hand
and i must know it else he loves me not

Enter Hotspur's Servant.

HOTSPUR
is gilliams gone?

HOTSPUR'S SERVANT
he is / my lord / an hour ago
sir walter blunt / my lord / waits on your grace[210]

Exit Hotspur's Servant.

LADY PERCY
and comes he from the king?[211] what is it carries you away?

HOTSPUR
why / my horse / my love / my horse

LADY PERCY
i fear my brother mortimer doth stir
about his title and hath sent for you
to line his enterprise / but if you go

HOTSPUR
so far <u>on foot</u>[212] i shall be weary love

LADY PERCY
in faith / i'll break thy little finger harry
if thou wilt not tell me all things true

HOTSPUR
love / i love thee not / this is no world
to play with mammets and to tilt with lips
we must have bloody noses and cracked crowns
and pass them current too

LADY PERCY
                              do you not love me?
nay tell me if <u>you speak</u>[213] in jest or no

HOTSPUR
come / wilt thou see me ride?
and when i am on horseback i will swear
i love thee infinitely / but hark you kate
i must not have you henceforth question me
<u>whither</u> i go / nor reason whereabout
<u>whither</u>[214] i must / i must / and to conclude
this evening must i leave you / <u>but</u>[215] gentle kate
whither i go / thither shall you go too
tonight will i set forth / will this content you?

LADY PERCY
it must of force

<u>Enter Blunt, Northumberland and Worcester.</u>[216]

BLUNT
i come with gracious offers from the king
if you vouchsafe me hearing and respect

NORTHUMBERLAND
welcome sir walter blunt / and would to god
you were of our determination

BLUNT
the king hath sent to know
the nature of your griefs and whereupon
you conjure from the breast of civil peace
such bold hostility / teaching his duteous land
audacious cruelty / if that the king
have any way your good deserts forgot
which he confesseth to be manifold
he bids you name your griefs / and with all speed
you shall have your desires with interest
and pardon absolute / for yourself / and these
herein misled by your suggestion

HOTSPUR
the king is kind / and well we know the king
knows at what time to promise when to pay
my father / and lord worcester / and myself
did give him that same royalty he wears
my father / in kind heart and pity moved
swore him assistance and performed it too
and[217] when the lords and barons of the realm
perceived northumberland did lean to him
then more and less came in with cap and knee
his majesty[218] / as greatness knows itself
proceeded further / cut me off the heads
of all the favourites of the former[219] king
save edmund mortimer / who / as you know
king richard once proclaimed his natural heir[220]

BLUNT
i came not to hear this

HOTSPUR
                         then to the point

in short time after he deposed the king
soon after that deprived him of his life
disgraced me in my happy victories
sought to entrap me by intelligence
rated mine uncle from the council board
in rage dismissed my[221] father from the court
broke oath on oath / committed wrong on wrong
and / in conclusion / drove us to seek out
this head of safety and withal to pry
into his title / the which we find
too indirect for long continuance

BLUNT
shall i return this answer to the king?

HOTSPUR
not so / sir walter / we'll withdraw awhile

BLUNT
i would you would accept of grace and love

WORCESTER
and maybe so we shall

BLUNT

                          pray god[222] you do

TEN[223]

A road outside Coventry.

FALSTAFF
bardolph / get thee before to coventry / fill me a bottle of sack /
our soldiers shall march through

BARDOLPH
farewell captain

   Exit Bardolph.

FALSTAFF
if i be not ashamed of my soldiers i am a <u>pickled fish</u>[224] / i have
misused the <u>power of conscription</u>[225] damnably / i have got in
exchange for a hundred and fifty soldiers / three hundred and odd
pounds / i <u>conscript</u>[226] none but good householders / inquire me
out contracted bachelors / such as had <u>rather</u>[227] hear the devil than
a drum / such as fear the sound of gunshot worse than a struck
fowl / or a hurt wild-duck

i <u>recruit</u>[228] me none but such toasts-and-butter / with hearts in
their bellies no bigger than pins' heads / and they have bought out
their services / and now my whole charge consists such as indeed
were never soldiers but dishonest servingmen / younger sons to
younger brothers / the cankers of a calm world and a long peace /
ten times more <u>dishonourably</u>[229] ragged than an old <u>tattered
flag</u>[230] / indeed / i had the most of them out of prison

<u>a mad fellow met me on the way and told me i had unloaded all
the gallows</u>[231] <u>and recruited</u>[232] <u>the dead bodies / no eye hath seen
such scarecrows / i'll not march through coventry with them /
that's flat</u>[233]

Enter Prince Harry.

PRINCE HARRY
how now / blown jack

FALSTAFF
what / hal / how now / mad wag / i thought your honour had
already been at shrewsbury

PRINCE HARRY[234]
'faith sir john / 'tis more than time that i were there / and you
too / but my powers are there already / the king <u>waits</u>[235] for us all /
we must away

FALSTAFF
tut / never fear me / i am as vigilant as a cat to steal cream

PRINCE HARRY
jack / whose fellows are these that come after?

FALSTAFF
mine hal / mine

PRINCE HARRY
i did never see such pitiful men

FALSTAFF
tut tut / good enough to toss / food for powder / food for
powder / they'll fill a pit as well as better / tush man / mortal
men / mortal men

PRINCE HARRY[236]
ay / but sir john / methinks they are exceeding poor / and bare /
too beggarly

FALSTAFF
'faith / for their poverty i know not where they had that / and for
their bareness / i am sure they never learned that of me

PRINCE HARRY
no i'll be sworn / sirrah make haste / hotspur[237] is already in the
field

FALSTAFF
what / is the king encamped?

PRINCE HARRY
he is jack / i fear we shall stay too long

FALSTAFF
well / to the latter end of a fray and the beginning of a feast
suits[238] a dull fighter and a keen guest

ELEVEN[239]

Rebel camp.

HOTSPUR
well said my noble scot / if speaking truth
in this fine age were not thought flattery
such attribution should the douglas have
by god[240] i cannot flatter / i do defy
the tongues of soothers but a braver place
in my heart's love hath no man than yourself

DOUGLAS
thou art the king of honour
no man so potent breathes upon the ground

Enter Messenger.

HOTSPUR
how does my father?[241] comes he not himself?

MESSENGER
he cannot come / my lord / he is grievous sick

HOTSPUR
how has he the leisure to be sick
in such a jostling time / who leads his power?
under whose government come they along?

MESSENGER
his letters bear his mind / not i / my lord

WORCESTER
i prithee / tell me / doth he keep his bed?

MESSENGER
he does[242] / my lord
at the time of my departure thence
he was much feared by his physicians

WORCESTER
his health was never better worth than now

HOTSPUR
sick now / droop now / this sickness doth infect
the very lifeblood of our enterprise
'tis catching hither / even to our camp
yet doth he give us bold advertisement
that with our small conjunction we should on
to see how fortune is disposed to us
for / as he writes / there is no quailing now
because the king is certainly possessed
of all our purposes / what say you to it?

WORCESTER
your father's sickness is a maim to us

HOTSPUR
a perilous gash / a very limb lopped off
and yet in faith it is not / his present want
seems more than we shall find it / were it good
to set the exact wealth of all our states
all at one cast? to set so rich a main
on the nice hazard of one doubtful hour?

WORCESTER
but yet i would your father had been here
this absence of your father's draws a curtain
that shows the ignorant a kind of fear
before not dreamt of / <u>it will be thought
by those</u>[243] <u>that know not why he is away
that wisdom / loyalty / and mere dislike
of our proceedings kept him in his bed</u>[244]

HOTSPUR
you strain too far
i rather of his absence make this use
it lends a lustre and more great opinion
a larger dare to our great enterprise
than if the earl were here / for men must think
if we without his help can make a head
to push against a kingdom / with his help
we shall overturn it topsy-turvy down
yet all goes well / yet all our joints are whole

DOUGLAS
as heart can think / there is not such a word
spoke of in scotland as[245] this term of fear

Enter Vernon.

HOTSPUR
sir richard[246] vernon / welcome by my soul

VERNON
pray god my news be worth a welcome / lord
the royal army[247] seven thousand strong
is coming hitherwards / with him prince john

HOTSPUR
no harm / what more?

VERNON
                         and further i have learned
the king himself in person is[248] set forth
or hitherwards intended speedily
with strong and mighty preparation

HOTSPUR
he shall be welcome too / where is his son
the nimble-footed madcap prince of wales
and all his friends that daffed the world aside
and bid it pass?

VERNON
                    all furnished / all in arms

HOTSPUR
no more / no more / they're all welcome[249]
they come like sacrifices in their trim
and to the fire-eyed maid of smoky war
all hot and bleeding will we offer them
o that mortimer[250] were come

VERNON
he cannot draw his power

DOUGLAS
that's the worst tidings that i hear of yet

HOTSPUR
what may the king's whole battle reach unto?

VERNON
to thirty thousand

HOTSPUR
        forty let it be
my father and <u>mortimer</u>[251] being both away
the powers of us may serve so great a day
<u>but gentlemen / the time of life is short</u>
<u>to spend that shortness basely were too long</u>
<u>if life did ride upon a dial's point</u>
<u>still ending at the arrival of an hour</u>
<u>if we live / we live to tread on kings</u>
<u>if die / brave death when princes die with us</u>[252]

TWELVE[253]

Royal camp.

KING HENRY IV
how bloodily the sun begins to peer
above yon <u>bulky</u>[254] hill / the day looks pale
at his distemperature

PRINCE HARRY
        the southern wind
doth play the trumpet to his purposes
and by <u>his</u>[255] hollow whistling in the leaves
foretells a tempest and a blustering day

KING HENRY IV
then with the losers let it sympathise
for nothing can seem foul to those that win

Enter Worcester and Vernon.

how now my lord of worcester / 'tis not well
that you and i should meet upon such terms
as now we meet / you have deceived our trust

WORCESTER
i have not sought the day of this dislike

KING HENRY IV
you have not sought it / how comes it then?

FALSTAFF
rebellion lay in his way and he found it

PRINCE HARRY
peace

WORCESTER
it pleased your majesty to turn your looks
of favour from myself and all our house
and yet i must remember you / my lord
we were the first and dearest of your friends
that is[256] / myself / my brother and his son
in richard's time / you swore to us
and you did swear that oath at doncaster
that you did claim no further than your right
the seat of gaunt / dukedom of lancaster
to this we swore our aid / but in short space
it rained down fortune showering on your head
and such a flood of greatness fell on you
what with our help / what with the absent king
what with the injuries of a wanton time
you took occasion to be quickly wooed
to take the royal sceptre[257] into your hand
forget[258] your oath to us at doncaster
and being fed by us / you used us so
that even our love durst not come near your sight
for fear of swallowing / but with nimble wing
we were enforced for safety sake to fly
out of sight / and raise this present head
whereby we stand opposed by such means

as you yourself have forged against yourself
by unkind usage / dangerous countenance
and violation of all faith and <u>truth</u>[259]

PRINCE HARRY
the prince of wales doth join with all the world
in praise of henry percy / by my hopes
i do not think a braver gentleman
more active-valiant or more valiant-young
more daring or more bold is now alive
for my part / i may speak it to my shame
i have a truant been to chivalry
and so i hear he doth account me too
<u>but</u>[260] <u>in your armies there is many a soul</u>
<u>shall pay full dearly for this encounter</u>
<u>if once they join in trial / tell your nephew</u>[261]
<u>i</u>[262] will / to save the blood on either side
try fortune with him in a single fight

KING HENRY IV
and prince of wales so dare we venture thee
albeit considerations infinite
do make against it / no / good / worcester / no
we love our people well / even those we love
that are misled upon your cousin's part
and will they take the offer of our grace
both he / and they / and you / yea every man
shall be my friend again and i'll be his
so / tell your cousin and bring me word
what he will do / but if he will not yield
rebuke and dread correction wait on us
and they shall do their office / so be gone
we will not now be troubled with reply
we offer fair / take it advisedly

Exeunt Worcester and Vernon.

PRINCE HARRY
it will not be accepted / on my life
this douglas / and then hotspur / both together
are confident against the world in arms

KING HENRY IV
hence therefore every leader to his charge
for <u>regardless of</u>[263] their answer will we set on them
and <u>god</u>[264] befriend us as our cause is just

Exeunt all except Prince Harry and Falstaff.

FALSTAFF
hal / if you see me down in the battle and <u>stand over</u>[265] me so / 'tis
a point of friendship

PRINCE HARRY
nothing but a colossus can do thee that friendship / say thy prayers
and farewell

FALSTAFF
i would 'twere bedtime hal / and all well

PRINCE HARRY
why / thou owest <u>god</u>[266] a death

FALSTAFF
'tis not due yet / i would be loath to pay him before his day / well
'tis no matter / honour pricks me on

<u>Exit Prince Harry.</u>[267]

yea / but how if honour prick me off when i come on? how then?
can honour set a leg? no / or an arm? no / or take away the grief
of a wound? no / honour hath no skill in surgery then? no / what
is honour? a word / what is in that word 'honour'? what is that
honour? air / who hath it? he <u>who</u>[268] died on wednesday / doth
he feel it? no / doth he hear it? no / 'tis insensible then? yea / to
the dead / but will it not live with the living? no / why? detraction
will not suffer it / therefore i'll none of it / honour is a mere
scutcheon / and so ends my catechism

THIRTEEN[269]

<u>*On the battlefield.*</u>[270]

BLUNT
what is thy name that thus thou crossest me?
what honour dost thou seek upon my head?

DOUGLAS
know then my name is douglas
and i do haunt thee in the battle thus
because some tell me that thou art a king

BLUNT
they tell thee true

DOUGLAS
this sword hath ended many / and shall thee
unless thou yield thee as my prisoner

BLUNT
i was not born <u>to yield</u>[271] / thou proud scot

    They fight. Douglas kills Blunt. Enter Hotspur.

DOUGLAS
all's done / all's won / here breathless lies the king

HOTSPUR
where?

DOUGLAS
here

HOTSPUR
<u>here</u>[272] / douglas? no / i know this face full well / <u>his name was
blunt / a gallant knight he was</u>[273] / semblably furnished like the
king himself

DOUGLAS
a fool go with thy soul whither it goes

a borrowed title hast thou bought too dear
why didst thou tell me that thou wert a king?

HOTSPUR
the king hath many marching in his coats

DOUGLAS
i'll murder all his wardrobe piece by piece
until i meet the king

[***]

FALSTAFF
soft / who are you? sir walter blunt / there's honour for you /
here's no vanity / i am as hot as molten lead and as heavy too /
god²⁷⁴ keep lead out of me / i need no more weight than mine
own bowels / i have led my ragamuffins where they are peppered /
there's not three of my hundred-and-fifty left alive

Enter Prince Harry.

PRINCE HARRY
what / stand you idle here?

FALSTAFF
o hal / i prithee / give me leave to breathe a while

PRINCE HARRY
is it a time to jest and dally now?

Exit Prince Harry.

FALSTAFF
i like not such grinning honour as sir walter hath / give me life

[***]²⁷⁵

DOUGLAS
another king / they grow like hydra's heads
what art thou / that counterfeit'st the person of a king?

KING HENRY IV
the king himself who / douglas / grieves at heart

so many of his shadows thou hast met
and not the very king / i have two boys
seek percy and thyself about the field
but seeing thou fall'st on me so luckily
i will assay thee / <u>so</u>[276] defend thyself

DOUGLAS
i fear thou art another counterfeit
and yet / in faith / thou bear'st thee like a king

Enter Prince Harry and Prince John.

PRINCE HARRY
it is the prince of wales that threatens thee
who never promiseth / but he means to pay

Douglas flees.

cheerly my lord / how fares your grace?

KING HENRY IV
<u>harry / withdraw thyself / thou bleed'st too much</u>[277]
thou hast showed thou makest some tender of my life

PRINCE HARRY
o <u>god</u>[278] / they did me too much injury
that ever said i hearkened <u>for</u>[279] your death

Exit King Henry IV.

<u>PRINCE JOHN</u>[280]
now come my lord / i'll lead you to your tent

PRINCE HARRY
lead me / i do not need your help

Exit Prince John.

and <u>god</u>[281] forbid a shallow scratch should drive
the prince of wales from such a field as this

Enter Hotspur and <u>Falstaff</u>.[282]

HOTSPUR
if i mistake not / thou art <u>the prince of wales</u>[283]

PRINCE HARRY
thou speak'st as if i would deny my name

HOTSPUR
my name is harry percy

PRINCE HARRY
                    why then i <u>say</u>[284]
i am the prince of wales / and think not percy
to share with me in glory any more
two stars keep not their motion in one sphere
nor can one england brook a double reign

HOTSPUR
<u>nor</u>[285] shall it harry / for the hour is come
to end the one of us / and would to <u>god</u>[286]
thy name in arms were now as great as mine

PRINCE HARRY
i'll make it greater ere i part from thee

HOTSPUR
i can no longer brook thy vanities

   They fight.

FALSTAFF
well said hal / to it hal / nay you shall find no boys' play here /
i can tell you

   Prince Harry kills Hotspur.

HOTSPUR
o harry / thou hast robbed me / of my youth
but thoughts / the slaves of life / and life / time's fool
and time / that takes survey of all the world
must have a stop / o i could prophesy
but that the <u>earthy</u>[287] and cold hand of death
lies on my tongue / no percy / thou art dust
and food for

Hotspur dies.

PRINCE HARRY
for worms / brave percy / fare thee well great heart
when that this body did contain a spirit
a kingdom for it was too small a bound
but now two paces of the vilest earth
is room enough / this earth that bears <u>thee dead</u>[288]
bears not alive so stout a gentleman
adieu / and take thy praise with thee to heaven

Prince Harry sees Falstaff on the ground.

what / old acquaintance / could not all this flesh
keep in a little life? poor jack / farewell
i could have better spared a better man
death hath not struck so <u>fat</u>[289] a deer today
though many dearer in this bloody fray
embowelled will i see thee by and by
till then / in blood / by noble percy lie

Exit Prince Harry.

Falstaff rises up.

FALSTAFF
embowelled / if you embowel me today i'll give you leave to
<u>embalm</u>[290] me / and eat me too tomorrow / 'sblood / 'twas time to
counterfeit / counterfeit? i lie / i am no counterfeit / to die is to be
a counterfeit / for he is but the counterfeit of a man who hath not
the life of a man / but to counterfeit dying when a man thereby
liveth is to be no counterfeit / but the true and perfect image of
life indeed / the better part of valour is discretion / in the which
better part i have saved my life

i am afraid of this gunpowder percy / though he be dead / how
if he should counterfeit too / and rise? by my faith / i am afraid
he would prove the better counterfeit / therefore i'll make him
sure / why may not he rise as well as i? nobody sees me / therefore
sirrah / with a new wound in your thigh

Falstaff stabs Hotspur.

Enter Prince Harry and Prince John.

PRINCE JOHN
did you not tell me this fat man was dead?

PRINCE HARRY
i did / i saw him / dead / breathless / and bleeding on the ground /
are you alive?

FALSTAFF
there is percy / if your father will do me any honour / so / if not
let him kill the next percy himself / i look to be either earl or
duke / i can assure you

PRINCE HARRY
why / percy i killed myself / and saw thee dead

FALSTAFF
did you? lord / lord / how <u>this</u>[291] world is given to lying / i grant
you i was down / and out of breath / and so was he / but we
rose / both at an instant / and fought a long hour by shrewsbury
clock / i'll <u>swear</u>[292] it upon my death / i gave him this wound in
the thigh / if the man were alive and would deny it / i would make
him eat a piece of my sword

PRINCE JOHN
this is the strangest tale that ever i heard

PRINCE HARRY
this is the strangest fellow / brother john
come / <u>bear</u>[293] your luggage nobly / on your back
for my part / if a lie may do thee grace
i'll gild it with the happiest terms i have

PRINCE JOHN
<u>fare you well falstaff / i in my condition</u>
<u>shall better speak of you than you deserve</u>[294]

Exeunt Prince Harry and Prince John.

FALSTAFF
<u>i would you had but the wit</u>[295] / i'll follow / as they say / for
reward / he that rewards me / god reward him / if i do grow great /

i'll grow less / i'll purge / i'll leave sack / and live cleanly / as a
nobleman should

[***][296]

King Henry IV and Warwick.

KING HENRY IV
thus ever did rebellion find rebuke
the trumpet sounds retreat / the day is ours[297]
bear worcester to the death / and vernon too
other offenders we will pause upon
rebellion in this land shall lose his sway[298]
meeting the check of such another day

King Henry IV collapses.

WARWICK
bring help / his majesty is grievous sick[299]

FOURTEEN[300]

FALSTAFF

a good sherry[301] sack hath a two-fold operation in it / it ascends me into the brain / dries me there all the foolish and dull vapours which environ it / makes it apprehensive / quick / full of nimble fiery and delectable shapes which delivered o'er to the voice / the tongue / becomes excellent wit

the second property of your excellent sherry is the warming of the blood / which before cold and settled and pale / which is the badge of cowardice / but the sherry warms it and makes it course from the inwards to the parts extreme / it illumineth the face which / as a beacon / gives warning to all the rest of this little kingdom man to arm / and then the commoners and inland petty spirits muster me all to their captain the heart / who great and puffed up with this[302] retinue / doth any deed of courage / and this valour comes of sack[303]

thereof comes it that prince harry is valiant / for the cold blood he did naturally inherit of his father he hath / like lean / sterile and bare land / manured / husbanded and tilled with excellent endeavour of drinking good and fertile sack[304] / if i had a thousand sons / the first humane principle i would teach them should be to forswear thin potations and to addict themselves to sack

FIFTEEN[305]

Northumberland.

NORTHUMBERLAND
gentle daughter / my honour is at pawn
and bar my going / nothing can redeem it

LADY PERCY
o yet for god's[306] sake / go not to these wars
the time was / father / that[307] you broke your word
when you were far more bound to it than now
when your own hotspur[308] / when my heart's dear harry
threw many a northward look to see his father
bring up his power / but he did long in vain
who then persuaded you to stay at home?
there were two honours lost / yours and your son's
for yours / it crumpled with my husband's corpse
for his / it shone from him / and by his light
did all the chivalry of england move
to do brave acts / he was indeed the glass
wherein the noble youth did dress themselves
to seem like him / so that in speech / in gait
in diet / in affections of delight
in military rules / humours of blood
he was the mark and glass / copy and book
that fashioned others / and him / o wondrous him
o miracle of men / him did you leave
to look upon the hideous god of war
in disadvantage / to abide a field
where nothing but the sound of hotspur's name
did seem defensible / so you left him
never / o never / do his ghost wrong
to hold your honour more precise / and nice
with others than with him

SIXTEEN[309]

FALSTAFF
giant / what says the doctor to my water?

PAGE
he said / sir / the water itself was a good healthy water / but for the
party that owed it / he might have more diseases than he knew of

FALSTAFF
men of all sorts take a pride to gibe at me / i am not only witty in
myself but the cause that wit is in other men

Enter Lord Chief Justice.

PAGE
sir / here comes the nobleman that the prince struck about
bardolph[310]

FALSTAFF
i will not see him

LORD CHIEF JUSTICE[311]
sir john falstaff

FALSTAFF
tell him i am deaf

PAGE
you must speak louder / my master is deaf

LORD CHIEF JUSTICE
i am sure he is / to the hearing of anything good
sir john falstaff / a word with you

FALSTAFF
my good lord / god give your lordship good time of day / i am
glad to see your lordship abroad / i heard say your lordship was
sick / and i must humbly beseech your lordship to have a reverent
care of your health

LORD CHIEF JUSTICE
sir john / i sent for you before your expedition to shrewsbury

FALSTAFF
an't please your lordship / i hear his majesty is returned from wales
with some discomfort

LORD CHIEF JUSTICE
i talk not of his majesty / you would not come when i sent for you

FALSTAFF
this apoplexy is / as i take it / a kind of deafness

LORD CHIEF JUSTICE
i think you are fallen into it[312] / for you hear not what i say to you

FALSTAFF
very well / my lord / very well / rather / an't please you / it is the
disease of not listening that i am troubled with

LORD CHIEF JUSTICE
to punish you would amend the attention of your ears / i sent for
you when there were matters against you for your life / to come
speak with me

FALSTAFF
as i was then advised by my learned counsel in law / i did not
come

LORD CHIEF JUSTICE
well the truth is / sir john / you live in great infamy

FALSTAFF
he that buckles him in my belt cannot live in less

LORD CHIEF JUSTICE
you have misled the youthful prince

FALSTAFF
the young prince hath misled me

LORD CHIEF JUSTICE
well / i am loath to gall a new-healed wound / your day's service

at shrewsbury hath a little gilded over your night's exploit on gad's
hill / you may thank the unquiet time for your quiet o'er-posting
that action

FALSTAFF
my lord

LORD CHIEF JUSTICE
you follow the young prince up and down like his ill angel

FALSTAFF
not so my lord / virtue is of so little regard in these <u>apple-sellers'</u>[313]
times / you that are old consider not the capacities of us that are
young

LORD CHIEF JUSTICE
do you set down your name in the scroll of youth that are written
down old with all the characters of age? have you not a moist eye?
a dry hand? a yellow cheek? a white beard? a decreasing leg? an
increasing belly? is not your voice broken? your wind short? your
chin double? your wit single? and every part about you blasted
with antiquity? and will you yet call yourself young?

FALSTAFF
my lord / i was born about three of the clock in the afternoon with
<u>white hair</u>[314] / and something a round belly / the truth is i am only
old in judgement and understanding / for the box of the ear that
the prince gave you / he gave it like a rude prince / and you took it
like a sensible lord / i have checked him for it / and the young lion
repents

LORD CHIEF JUSTICE
well / <u>god</u>[315] send the prince a better companion

FALSTAFF
<u>god</u>[316] send the companion a better prince / i cannot rid my hands
of him

LORD CHIEF JUSTICE
well / the king hath severed you and prince harry / i hear you
are going with <u>prince john against the rebels</u>[317] and the earl of
northumberland

FALSTAFF
yea / there is not a dangerous action can peep out his head but
i am thrust upon it / well / i cannot last forever / it was always yet
the trick of our english nation / if they have a good thing to make
it too common / if ye will needs say i am an old man / you should
give me rest / i would to god my name were not so terrible to the
enemy as it is

LORD CHIEF JUSTICE
well / be honest / be honest / and <u>god</u>[318] bless your expedition

FALSTAFF
will your lordship lend me a thousand pound / to furnish me
forth?

LORD CHIEF JUSTICE
not a penny / not a penny / fare you well

Exit Lord Chief Justice.

FALSTAFF
what money is in my purse?

PAGE
seven groats and two pence

FALSTAFF
i can get no remedy against this consumption of the purse /
borrowing only lingers and lingers it out but the disease is
incurable

a pox of this gout / or a gout of this pox / for the one or the other
plays the rogue with my great toe / 'tis no matter if i do limp /
i have the wars for my colour and my pension shall seem the more
reasonable / a good wit will make use of anything / i will turn
diseases to advantage

<u>Enter Sheriff, Snare and Mistress Quickly.</u>[319]

SHERIFF[320]
we must arrest sir john falstaff

MISTRESS QUICKLY
i am undone by him / i warrant you / he's an infinitive thing upon
my score / since my case[321] is so openly known to the world / let
him be brought in to his answer / a hundred mark is a long one
for a poor lone woman to bear / and i have borne / and borne /
and borne / and have been fubbed off / and fubbed off / and
fubbed off / from this day to that day that it is a shame to be
thought on / do me your offices / do your offices / master fang and
master snare / do me / do me / do me your offices

FALSTAFF
how now / whose mare's dead? what's the matter?

SHERIFF
sir john / i arrest you at the suit of mistress quickly

FALSTAFF
away varlets / bardolph / cut me off the villain's head / throw the
quean in the channel

MISTRESS QUICKLY
throw me in the channel / i'll throw thee in the channel / wilt
thou? wilt thou? thou bastardly rogue / murder / murder / wilt
thou kill the king's officers?[322]

FALSTAFF
keep them off bardolph

SHERIFF
a rescue / a rescue

MISTRESS QUICKLY
good people bring a rescue or two

FALSTAFF[323]
away you scullion / you rampallion

Enter Lord Chief Justice.

LORD CHIEF JUSTICE
what is the matter? keep the peace

MISTRESS QUICKLY
good / my lord / be good to me / i beseech you stand to me

LORD CHIEF JUSTICE
how now sir john / what are you brawling here?
doth this become your place / your time and business?

MISTRESS QUICKLY
most worshipful lord / an't please your grace / i am a poor widow
of eastcheap / and he is arrested at my suit

LORD CHIEF JUSTICE
for what sum?

MISTRESS QUICKLY
it is not[324] for some my lord / it is for all / all i have / he hath eaten
me out of house and home / he hath put all my substance into
that fat belly of his / but i will have some of it out again

LORD CHIEF JUSTICE
how comes this sir john? are you not ashamed to enforce a poor
widow to so rough a course to come by her own?

FALSTAFF
what is the gross sum that i owe thee?

MISTRESS QUICKLY
marry / if thou wert an honest man / thyself and the money
too / thou didst swear to me upon a parcel-gilt goblet / sitting
in my dolphin-chamber / at the round table / by a sea-coal fire /
upon wednesday in whitsun[325] week / when the prince broke
thy head for liking his father to a singing-man of windsor / thou
didst swear to me then / as i was washing thy wound / to marry
me / and make me my lady thy wife / can you deny it? did not
goodwife keech the butcher's wife come in then / calling[326] me
gossip quickly? coming in to borrow a mess of vinegar / telling us
she had a good dish of prawns / whereby thou didst desire to eat
some / whereby i told thee they were ill for a new[327] wound? and
did you not when she was gone downstairs / desire me to be no
more so familiarity[328] with such poor people / saying that ere long
they should call me m'lady? and didst thou not kiss me and bid

me fetch thee thirty shillings? i put thee now to thy oath / deny it
if thou canst

FALSTAFF
my lord / this is a poor mad soul / and she says up and down the
town that her eldest son is like you / she hath been in good case /
and the truth is / poverty hath distracted her / but for these foolish
officers / i beseech you / i may have redress against them

LORD CHIEF JUSTICE
sir john / sir john / i am well acquainted with your manner of
wrenching the true cause the false way / you have / as it appears to
me / practised upon the easy-yielding spirit of this woman / and
made her serve your uses / both in purse and in person

MISTRESS QUICKLY
yea / in truth my lord

LORD CHIEF JUSTICE
pray thee peace / pay her the debt you owe her / and unpay the
villainy you have done her / the one you may do with sterling
money and the other with current repentance

   Enter Harcourt.[329]

LORD CHIEF JUSTICE
what's the matter?

HARCOURT[330]
the king / my lord

FALSTAFF
as i am a gentleman

MISTRESS QUICKLY
faith / you said so before

FALSTAFF
as i am a gentleman / come no more words of it

MISTRESS QUICKLY
by this heavenly ground i tread on i must be fain to pawn my
silverware / and the tapestry of my dining-chambers

FALSTAFF
come / if it[331] were not for thy humours / there's not a better
wench in england / go wash thy face and withdraw[332] the action /
come thou must not be in this humour with me / do you not
know me? come / come / i know you were set up to this / let it be
ten pounds / if you can[333]

MISTRESS QUICKLY
pray thee / sir john / let it be but six pounds[334] / i'faith i am loath
to pawn my silver / so god save me

FALSTAFF
let it alone / i'll make other shift / you'll be a fool still

MISTRESS QUICKLY
well / you shall have it / though i pawn my gown / i hope you'll
come to supper / you'll pay me all together?

FALSTAFF
do[335] i live?

MISTRESS QUICKLY
will you have doll tearsheet at supper?

FALSTAFF
no more words / let's have her

Exeunt Mistress Quickly, Sheriff and Fang.

bardolph / go with her / hook on / hook on[336]

Exit Bardolph.

LORD CHIEF JUSTICE
i have heard better[337] news

FALSTAFF
what's the news my lord?

LORD CHIEF JUSTICE
where lay the king last night?[338]

HARCOURT[339]
at westminster[340] / my lord

FALSTAFF
i hope / my lord / all's well / what is the news my lord?

LORD CHIEF JUSTICE
come all his forces back?

HARCOURT[341]
no / fifteen hundred foot / five hundred horse
are marched up to prince john[342] of lancaster
against northumberland and the rebel power[343]

FALSTAFF
comes the king back from wales / my noble lord?

LORD CHIEF JUSTICE
sir john / you loiter here too long / being you are to take soldiers
up in gloucestershire as you go[344]

FALSTAFF
will you sup with me master harcourt?[345]

LORD CHIEF JUSTICE
what foolish master taught you these manners / sir john?

FALSTAFF
master harcourt[346] / this is the right fencing grace / tap for tap /
and so part fair

LORD CHIEF JUSTICE
now the lord lighten thee / thou art a great fool

SEVENTEEN[347]

PRINCE HARRY
<u>before god</u>[348] / i am exceeding weary

POINS
is't come to that? i had thought weariness durst not have attached
<u>to</u>[349] one of so high blood

PRINCE HARRY
'faith / it does me / does it not show <u>vilely</u>[350] in me to desire small
beer?

POINS
why / a prince should not remember so weak a composition

PRINCE HARRY
belike then my appetite was not princely got / but indeed these
humble considerations make me out of love with my greatness /
what a disgrace is it to me to remember thy name / or to know thy
face tomorrow / shall i tell thee one thing poins?

POINS
yes faith / and let it be an excellent good thing

PRINCE HARRY
i tell thee it is not <u>right</u>[351] that i should be sad now my father is
sick / albeit i could tell thee as to one it pleases me / for fault of a
better / to call my friend / i could be sad / and sad indeed too

POINS
very <u>hard</u>[352] / upon such a subject

PRINCE HARRY
by this hand thou thinkest me as far in the devil's book as thou
and falstaff / let the end try the man / but i tell thee my heart
bleeds inwardly that my father is so sick / and keeping such
vile company as thou art / hath in reason taken from me all
ostentation of sorrow

POINS
the reason?

PRINCE HARRY
what wouldst thou think of me if i should weep?

POINS
i would think thee a most princely hypocrite

PRINCE HARRY
it would be every man's thought / and what accites your most
worshipful thought to think so?

POINS
why / because you have been so lewd / and so much engraffed to
falstaff

PRINCE HARRY
and to thee

POINS
by this light i am well spoke on / i can hear it with my own ears /
the worst that they can say of me is that i am a second brother /
and that i am a proper fellow of my hands / and those two things
i confess i cannot help

   Enter Bardolph.

BARDOLPH
god save your grace

PRINCE HARRY
and yours / most noble bardolph / and how doth thy master?

BARDOLPH
well / my lord / he heard of your grace's coming to town / there's a
letter for you

POINS
delivered with good respect / and how doth the <u>hog roast</u>[353] / your
master?

BARDOLPH
in bodily health sir

POINS
marry / the immortal part needs a physician

PRINCE HARRY
i do allow this wen to be as familiar with me as my dog / <u>look</u>[354]
you how he writes

POINS (*reads*)
'john falstaff knight' / every man must know that / as oft as he has
occasion to name himself / <u>'sir john falstaff knight / to the son of
the king nearest his father / harry / prince of wales / greeting'</u>[355] /
why this is a certificate

PRINCE HARRY (*reads*)
'i commend me to thee / i commend thee and i leave thee / be not
too familiar with poins for he misuses thy favours so much that
he swears thou art to marry his sister nell / repent at idle times
as thou mayest / and so farewell / thine as thou usest him / jack
falstaff with my familiars / john with my brothers and sisters / and
sir john with all europe'

POINS
my lord / i'll steep this letter in sack and make him eat it

PRINCE HARRY
thus we play the fools with the time / and the spirits of the wise sit
in the clouds and mock us / is your master here in london?

BARDOLPH
yea my lord

PRINCE HARRY
where sups he tonight? doth the old boar feed in the old <u>trough</u>?[356]

BARDOLPH
at the old place my lord in eastcheap / <u>with</u>[357] old mistress
quickly / and mistress doll tearsheet

PRINCE HARRY
shall we steal upon them ned / at supper?

POINS
i am your shadow my lord / i'll follow you

PRINCE HARRY
bardolph / no word to your master that i am yet come to town /
there's for your silence

BARDOLPH
i have no tongue sir

PRINCE HARRY
fare you well

Exit Bardolph.

this doll tearsheet should be some <u>whore</u>[358]

POINS
as common as the <u>road</u>[359] between saint alban's and london

PRINCE HARRY
how might we see falstaff tonight in his true colours and not
ourselves be seen?

POINS
put on two <u>aprons</u>[360] and wait upon him at his table <u>as</u>[361]
<u>servants</u>[362]

PRINCE HARRY
from a prince to a prentice? a low transformation / that shall be
mine / <u>but do you use me thus ned? must i marry your sister?</u>[363]

POINS
<u>god send the wench</u>[364] no worse fortune / but i never said so

EIGHTEEN[365]

Boar's Head Tavern.

FRANCIS[366]
what the devil hast thou brought there? apples?[367] thou knowest sir
john cannot endure an apple-john

SECOND DRAWER
dispatch / the room where they supped is too hot / they'll come in
straight

MISTRESS QUICKLY
i'faith sweetheart methinks now you are in an excellent good
temporality / your pulsidge beats as extraordinarily as heart would
desire / and your colour i warrant you is as red as any rose / in
good truth / but i'faith you have drunk too much canaries / and
that's a marvellous searching wine and it perfumes the blood ere
one can say 'what's this?' how do you now?

DOLL TEARSHEET
better than i was / hem

MISTRESS QUICKLY
why / that's well said / a good heart's worth gold / here comes sir
john

Enter Falstaff.

FALSTAFF
empty the jordan / how now mistress doll

MISTRESS QUICKLY
sick / yea good faith

FALSTAFF
so is all her sort[368] / they are sick

DOLL TEARSHEET
you muddy bastard[369] / is that all the comfort you give me? hang
yourself / you muddy conger / hang yourself

MISTRESS QUICKLY
by my troth / this is the old fashion / you two never meet but you
fall to some discord / you are both as rheumatic as two dry toasts /
you cannot bear with one another's confirmities / one must bear
and that must be you / you are the weaker vessel / as they say / the
emptier vessel

DOLL TEARSHEET
can a weak empty vessel bear such a huge full <u>barrel</u>?[370] come i'll be
friends with thee jack / thou art going to the wars / and whether
i shall ever see thee again or no / there is nobody cares

<u>FRANCIS</u>[371]
sir / pistol's below and would speak with you

DOLL TEARSHEET
hang him / swaggering rascal / let him not come hither / it is the
foul-mouthed'st rogue in england

MISTRESS QUICKLY
if he swagger let him not come here / no / by my faith / i must live
<u>among</u>[372] my neighbours / shut the door i pray you

FALSTAFF
he's no swaggerer hostess / a tame cheater / you may stroke him as
gently as a puppy greyhound / call him up

   Exit Francis.

MISTRESS QUICKLY
cheater call you him? i will bar no honest man nor no cheater /
but i do not love swaggering by my troth / <u>look you how i shake /
feel you how i shake</u>[373] / an 'twere an aspen leaf

   Enter Pistol.

PISTOL
god save you sir john

FALSTAFF
welcome pistol / here pistol i charge you with a cup of sack / do
you discharge upon mine hostess

PISTOL
i will discharge upon her sir john with two bullets

FALSTAFF
she is pistol-proof sir

MISTRESS QUICKLY
come / i'll drink no more than will do me good / for no man's
pleasure

PISTOL
then to you / mistress <u>doll</u>[374] / i will charge you

DOLL TEARSHEET
charge me / what / you poor base rascally cheating lack-linen
scoundrel / you mouldy rogue / away / i am meat for your master

PISTOL
i know you mistress <u>doll</u>[375]

DOLL TEARSHEET
away you cut-purse rascal

PISTOL
i will murder your ruff for this

FALSTAFF
no more pistol / i would not have you go off here / discharge
yourself of our company

MISTRESS QUICKLY
no / good captain pistol / not here / sweet captain

DOLL TEARSHEET
captain / thou abominable damned cheater / art thou not ashamed
to be called captain? if captains were of my mind they would
truncheon you out for taking their names upon you before
you have earned them / you / a captain? you / for what? / he /
a captain? hang him / <u>by this wine i'll thrust my knife in your
mouldy chaps an you play the saucy cuttle with me</u>[376]

BARDOLPH
pray thee go down good <u>ensign</u>[377]

FALSTAFF
hark thee hither mistress doll

PISTOL
i'll be revenged of her

MISTRESS QUICKLY[378]
pray thee go down / 'tis very late i'faith

PISTOL
i'll see her damned first / and let the welkin roar / shall we fall foul
for toys?

MISTRESS QUICKLY
for god's sake / be quiet

PISTOL
then feed and be fat / come / give 's some sack / and sweetheart lie
thou there

FALSTAFF
pistol / i would be quiet

PISTOL
sweet knight / i kiss thy neaf / what / we have seen the seven stars

DOLL TEARSHEET
for god's sake / thrust him downstairs

PISTOL
thrust him downstairs?

BARDOLPH
come get you downstairs

PISTOL
what / shall we have incision? shall we imbrue?

Falstaff fights Pistol.

MISTRESS QUICKLY
here's goodly stuff toward

DOLL TEARSHEET
i pray thee jack / i pray thee / do not draw

FALSTAFF
get you downstairs

MISTRESS QUICKLY
murder / i warrant now / put up your naked weapons / put up
your naked weapons

> *Exit Pistol <u>dragged out by Francis, Second Drawer and
> Bardolph</u>.*[379]

FALSTAFF
<u>throw</u>[380] <u>him down bardolph / if he do nothing but speak
nothing / he shall be nothing here</u>[381]

DOLL TEARSHEET
i pray thee jack / be quiet / the rascal's gone / ah you whoreson
little valiant villain you

MISTRESS QUICKLY
are you not hurt? <u>methought he</u>[382] made a shrewd thrust at your
belly

> *Enter Bardolph.*

FALSTAFF
have you turned him out o' doors?

BARDOLPH
yea sir / you have hurt him sir

FALSTAFF
to brave me

DOLL TEARSHEET
ah you sweet little rogue / alas poor ape / how you sweat / come
let me wipe thy face / come on you whoreson chops / ah rogue /
i'faith i love thee / ah villain

FALSTAFF
a rascally slave / sit on my knee doll / a rascal bragging slave / the
rogue fled from me

DOLL TEARSHEET
thou whoreson little tidy bartholomew boar-pig / when will you
leave fighting o'days and <u>thrusting</u>[383] o'nights and begin to patch
up your old body for heaven?

Enter Prince Harry and Poins disguised as drawers.

FALSTAFF
peace doll / do not speak like a death's head / do not bid me
remember mine end

DOLL TEARSHEET
sirrah / what humour's the prince of?

FALSTAFF
a good shallow young fellow / would have made a good <u>pantry
boy</u>[384] / would <u>have</u>[385] chipp'd bread well

DOLL TEARSHEET
they say poins has a good wit

FALSTAFF
he a good wit? hang him / baboon / he's as thick as tewkesbury
mustard / there's no more wit in him than is in a mallet

DOLL TEARSHEET
why does the prince love him so then?

FALSTAFF
because their legs are both of a thickness / he plays at <u>games</u>[386]
well / rides the wild-mare with the boys / jumps upon joined-
stools / swears / a weak mind and an able body / for the which the
prince admits him / for <u>he</u>[387] himself is such another

PRINCE HARRY
would not this <u>knave</u>[388] have his ears cut off?

POINS
let's beat him before his whore

PRINCE HARRY
look <u>whether</u>[389] the withered elder hath not his <u>head</u>[390] clawed like
a parrot

POINS
is it not strange that desire should so many years outlive
performance?

Doll kisses Falstaff.[391]

FALSTAFF
kiss me doll / you give me flattering <u>kisses</u>[392]

DOLL TEARSHEET
by my troth / i kiss thee with a most constant heart

FALSTAFF
i am old / i am old

DOLL TEARSHEET
i love thee better than i love ever a scurvy young boy of them all

FALSTAFF
what stuff will you have a <u>skirt</u>[393] made of? i shall receive money
on thursday / a merry song / come / it grows late / we'll to bed /
you'll forget me when i am gone

DOLL TEARSHEET
by my troth / thou'lt set me a-weeping an thou sayest so / prove
that / well / hearken at the end

FALSTAFF
some sack francis

<u>PRINCE HARRY</u>[394]
anon anon sir

FALSTAFF
ha? a bastard son of the king's?

PRINCE HARRY
why / thou globe of sinful continents / what a life dost thou lead?

FALSTAFF
better than you / i am a gentleman

PRINCE HARRY
very true sir

MISTRESS QUICKLY
o the lord[395] preserve thy good[396] grace / by my troth / welcome
back[397] to london / now the lord bless that sweet face of thine

FALSTAFF
thou whoreson mad compound of majesty / by this light flesh and
corrupt blood / thou art welcome

POINS
my lord / he will drive you out of your revenge and turn all to a
merriment

PRINCE HARRY
how vilely did you speak of me / even now before this honest /
virtuous / civil gentlewoman

MISTRESS QUICKLY
god's blessing of your good heart / and so she is by my troth

FALSTAFF
did you hear me?

PRINCE HARRY
yea and you knew me / as you did when you ran away at[398] gad's
hill / you knew i was at your back and spoke it on purpose to try
my patience

FALSTAFF
no / no / no / not so / i did not think you were within hearing

PRINCE HARRY
then confess the wilful abuse / and then i know how to handle you

FALSTAFF
no abuse hal / on mine honour / no abuse

PRINCE HARRY
no[399] / to dispraise me / and call me <u>pantry boy</u>[400] / and bread-
chipper / and i know not what

FALSTAFF
no abuse hal

POINS
no abuse?

FALSTAFF
no abuse ned / i'the world / honest ned / none / i dispraised him
before the wicked / that the wicked might not fall in love with
him / no abuse hal / none ned none / no / faith boys / none

PRINCE HARRY
is she of the wicked? is thine hostess here of the wicked? or honest
bardolph of the wicked?

POINS
answer / thou dead elm / answer

   Enter Peto.

PETO
my lord

PRINCE HARRY
peto

PETO
the king / your father / is at westminster
<u>you must away to court sir / now at once</u>[401]
<u>your father's servants</u>[402] <u>stay at door for you</u>[403]
and as i came along
i met and overtook a dozen captains
bare-headed / sweating / knocking at the taverns
and asking everyone for sir john falstaff

PRINCE HARRY
by heaven / poins / i feel me much to blame
so idly to profane the precious time
when tempest of commotion / like the south

borne with black vapour / doth begin to melt
and drop upon our bare unarmed heads
give me my coat[404] / and[405] falstaff / good night

Exeunt Prince Harry and Peto.

FALSTAFF
now comes in the sweetest morsel of the night and we must hence
and leave it unpicked

farewell doll / you see my good wenches how men of merit are
sought after / the undeserver may sleep when the man of action is
called on / farewell good wenches / if i be not sent away i will see
you again ere i go

DOLL TEARSHEET
i cannot speak / if my heart be not ready to burst / well sweet
jack / have a care of thyself

FALSTAFF
farewell / farewell

MISTRESS QUICKLY
well / fare thee well / i have known thee these twenty-nine years
come peascod time / but an honester and truer-hearted man /
well / fare thee well

Falstaff collapses.[406]

BARDOLPH
mistress tearsheet

MISTRESS QUICKLY
what's the matter?

BARDOLPH
good mistress tearsheet / come to my master

MISTRESS QUICKLY
o run / doll / run / run / good doll / come / she comes blubbered /
will you come doll

NINETEEN[407]

Westminster.

WARWICK
many good morrows to your majesty

KING HENRY IV
is it good morrow?

WARWICK
'tis one o'clock and past

KING HENRY IV
<u>do</u>[408] you perceive the body of our kingdom
how foul it is / what rank diseases grow
and with what danger near the heart of it?

WARWICK
it is but as a body yet distempered
which to his former strength may be restored
with good advice and little medicine
my lord / northumberland will soon be <u>quelled</u>[409]

KING HENRY IV
o <u>god</u>[410] / that one might read the book of fate
and see the revolution of the times
'tis not ten years gone / <u>i think you were by</u>[411]
when richard / with his eye brimful of tears
then checked and rated by northumberland
did speak these words / now proved a prophecy?
'northumberland thou ladder / by the which
my cousin bolingbroke ascends my throne'
though then <u>god</u>[412] knows i had no such intent
but that necessity so bowed the state
that i and greatness were compell'd to kiss
'the time shall come' / thus did he follow it
'the time will come that foul sin gathering head
shall break into corruption' / so went on

foretelling this same time's condition
and the division of our amity

WARWICK
there is a history in all men's lives
figuring the natures of the times deceased
the which observed / a man may prophesy
with a near aim of the main chance of things
king richard might create a perfect guess
that great northumberland / then false to him
would of that seed grow to greater falseness
which should not find a ground to root upon
unless on you

KING HENRY IV
they say the forces of[413] northumberland
are fifty thousand strong

WARWICK
                              it cannot be my lord
rumour doth double like the voice and echo
the numbers of the feared / please it your grace
to go to bed / upon my soul[414] my lord
the powers that you already have sent forth
shall bring this prize in very easily
your majesty hath been this fortnight ill
and these unseasoned hours perforce must add
unto your sickness

KING HENRY IV
                         i will take your counsel
and were these inward wars once out of hand
we would dear friend unto the holy land

TWENTY[415]

Gloucestershire.

SHALLOW
come on / come on / come on sir / give me your hand sir / give
me your hand sir / an early stirrer by the rood / and how doth my
good cousin silence?

SILENCE
good morrow / good cousin shallow

SHALLOW
and how doth your bedfellow? and your fairest daughter / my god-
daughter ellen? i dare say young william is become a good scholar /
he is at oxford still is he not?

SILENCE
indeed sir / to my cost

SHALLOW
he must then to the inns o' court shortly / i was once of clement's
inn where i think they will talk of mad shallow yet

SILENCE
you were called 'lusty shallow' then cousin

SHALLOW
by the mass / i was called anything / and i would have done
anything indeed too / and roundly too / there was i and little
john doit of staffordshire / and black george barnes / and francis
pickbone / and will squele / a <u>cotswold</u>[416] man / you had not four
such swinge-bucklers in all the inns o' court again / and i may say
to you / we knew where the bona-robas were / and had the best of
them all at commandment / then was jack falstaff / now sir john /
a boy and page to thomas mowbray duke of norfolk

SILENCE
this sir john / cousin / that comes hither today about soldiers?

SHALLOW
the same sir john / the very same / i <u>see</u>[417] him break scoggin's head
at the court gate / when he was a crack not thus high / and the
very same day did i fight with one sampson stockfish / a fruiterer
behind gray's inn / <u>jesu / jesu</u>[418] / the mad days that i have spent /
and to see how many of my old acquaintance are dead

SILENCE
we shall all follow cousin

SHADOW
certain / 'tis certain / very sure / very sure / death <u>as the psalmist
saith</u>[419] is certain to all / all shall die / how a good yoke of bullocks
at stamford fair?

SILENCE
by my troth / i was not there

SHALLOW
death is certain / is old <u>double</u>[420] of your town living yet?

SILENCE
dead sir

SHALLOW
jesu / jesu / dead / <u>he</u>[421] drew a good bow / and dead / <u>he</u>[422] shot a
fine shoot / dead / how a score of ewes now?

SILENCE
thereafter as they be / a score of good ewes may be worth ten pounds

SHALLOW
and is old <u>double</u>[423] dead?

Enter Davy and Falstaff.

DAVY
<u>beg pardon sir</u>[424]

SHALLOW
look / here comes good sir john / give me your good hand / give
me your worship's good hand / <u>by my troth</u>[425] you <u>look</u>[426] well /
and bear your years very well / welcome good sir john

FALSTAFF
i am glad to see you well / good master robert shallow / <u>one of the</u>
<u>king's justices of the peace</u>[427] / master <u>surecard</u>[428] as i think?

SHALLOW
no sir john / it is my cousin silence in commission with me

FALSTAFF
good master silence / it well befits you should be of the peace

SILENCE
your good worship is welcome

FALSTAFF
fie / this is hot weather gentlemen / have you provided me here
half a dozen sufficient men?

SHALLOW
marry / have we sir / will you sit? where's the roll? where's the roll?
where's the roll? let me see / let me see / let me see / so / so / yea /
here is two more called than your number

FALSTAFF
<u>these fellows will do well master shallow</u>[429]

SHALLOW
<u>and so / i pray you / go in with me to dinner</u>[430]

FALSTAFF
come / i will go drink with you / but i cannot tarry dinner / i am
glad to see you by my troth master shallow

SHALLOW
o sir john / do you remember since we lay all night in the
windmill in saint george's field?

FALSTAFF
no more of that / good master shallow / no more of that

SHALLOW
ha / <u>'twas</u>[431] a merry night / and is jane nightwork alive?

FALSTAFF
she lives / master shallow

SHALLOW
she never could away with me

FALSTAFF
never / never / she would always say she could not abide master
shallow

SHALLOW
by the mass / i could anger her to the heart / she was then a bona-
roba / doth she hold her own well?

FALSTAFF
old / old / master shallow

SHALLOW
nay she must be old / she cannot choose but be old / certain she's
old / she had robin nightwork by old nightwork before i came to
clement's inn

SILENCE
that's fifty-five year ago

SHALLOW
ha / cousin silence / that you had seen that that this knight and
i have seen / ha / sir john / said i well?

FALSTAFF
we have heard the chimes at midnight / master shallow

SHALLOW
that we have / that we have / that we have / in faith / sir john / we
have / our watchword was 'hem boys' / come let's to dinner / come
let's to dinner / jesus[432] the days that we have seen / come / come

Exeunt Shallow, Silence and Davy.

FALSTAFF
i will fetch off these justices / i do see the bottom of justice
shallow / lord / lord / how subject we old men are to this vice of
lying / this same starved justice hath done nothing but prate to

me of the wildness of his youth and the feats he hath done / and
every third word a lie / i do remember him at clement's inn / like a
man made after supper of a cheese-paring / when he was naked he
was for all the world like a forked radish with a head fantastically
carved upon it / he was the very genius of famine / yet lecherous as
a monkey / came ever in the rearward of the fashion / and now is
this become a squire / and now has he land and beefs / well i'll be
acquainted with him / if the young dace be a bait for the old pike /
i see no reason in the law of nature but i may snap at him / <u>i will
devise matter enough out of this shallow to keep prince harry in
continual laughter / o you shall see hal laugh till his face be like a
wet cloak ill laid up</u>[433] / let time shape and there an end

TWENTY-ONE[434]

KING HENRY IV
<u>where is my son? where is the prince of wales?</u>[435]

WARWICK[436]
i think he's gone to hunt / my lord / at windsor

KING HENRY IV
and how accompanied?

WARWICK
i do not know / my lord

KING HENRY IV
is not his brother thomas with him?

WARWICK
no / my good lord / he is in presence here

PRINCE THOMAS
what would my lord and father?

KING HENRY IV
why art thou not at windsor <u>now / with harry</u>[437]

PRINCE THOMAS
he is not there today / he dines in london

KING HENRY IV
and how accompanied? canst thou tell that?

PRINCE THOMAS
with poins / and other his continual followers

KING HENRY IV
the blood weeps from my heart when i do shape
in forms imaginary the unguided days
and rotten times that you shall look upon
when i am sleeping with my ancestors
for when his headstrong riot hath no curb
when rage and hot blood are his counsellors
when means and lavish manners meet together
o with what wings shall his affections fly
towards fronting peril and opposed decay

WARWICK
my gracious lord / you look beyond him quite
the prince but studies his companions
like a strange tongue / wherein / to gain the language
'tis needful that the most immodest word
be looked upon and learned

Enter Harcourt.

KING HENRY IV
how now[438] / what news?[439]

HARCOURT
from enemies / heaven keep your majesty
and when they stand against you / may they fall
as those that i am come to tell you of
prince john / your son / doth kiss your grace's hand[440]
northumberland has breathed his last / my lord[441]
there is not now a rebel's sword unsheathed
but peace puts forth her olive everywhere

KING HENRY IV
and wherefore should these good news make me sick?
will fortune never come with both hands full
but write her fair words still in foulest letters?
i should rejoice now at this happy news
and now my sight fails and my brain is giddy
o me / come near me now

He swoons.

HARCOURT[442]

comfort your majesty

PRINCE THOMAS
o my royal father / look up[443]

WARWICK
stand from him / give him air / he'll straight be well

PRINCE THOMAS
no / no / he cannot long hold out these pangs

WARWICK
speak lower / for the king recovers

KING HENRY IV
let there be no noise made / my gentle friends
unless some music for[444] my weary spirit

WARWICK
call for the music in the other room

Exit Harcourt.

KING HENRY IV
set me the crown upon my pillow here

PRINCE THOMAS
his eye is hollow and he changes much

WARWICK
less noise / less noise

Enter Prince Harry.

PRINCE HARRY
how now / rain within doors and none abroad
how doth the king?

PRINCE THOMAS[445]
                    exceeding ill

PRINCE HARRY
heard he the good news yet? tell it him

PRINCE THOMAS[446]
he altered much upon the hearing it

WARWICK
not so much noise / my lords / sweet prince / speak low
the king / your father / is disposed to sleep

PRINCE THOMAS
let us withdraw into the other room

WARWICK
will't please your grace to go along with us?

PRINCE HARRY
no / i will sit and watch here by the king

Exeunt all except Prince Harry and King Henry IV.

why doth the crown lie there upon his pillow
being so troublesome a bedfellow?
o polish'd perturbation / golden care
that keep'st the ports of slumber open wide
to many a watchful night / sleep with it now
yet not so sound and half so deeply sweet
as he whose brow with homely biggen bound
snores out the watch of night / my father
this sleep is sound / indeed this is a sleep
that from this golden <u>circle</u>[447] hath divorced
so many english kings / thy due from me
is tears and heavy sorrows of the blood
which nature / love / and filial tenderness

shall / o dear father / pay thee plenteously
my due from thee is this imperial crown
which as immediate <u>as</u>[448] thy place and blood
derives itself to me / <u>look</u>[449] <u>here</u>[450] it sits
which <u>god</u>[451] shall guard / and put the world's whole strength
into one giant arm / it shall not force
this lineal honour from me / this from thee
will i to mine leave / as 'tis left to me

King Henry IV awakens to see Prince Harry wearing the crown.

i never thought to hear you speak again

KING HENRY IV
thy wish was father / harry / to that thought
you seek the greatness that will o'erwhelm you
stay but a little / for my day is dim
thou hast stolen that which / after some few hours
were thine without offence / and at my death
thou hast sealed up my expectation
your life did manifest you loved me not
and you will have me die assured of it
then get thee gone / and dig my grave thyself
and bid the merry bells ring to thine ear
that thou art crowned / not that i am dead
pluck down my officers / break my decrees
for now a time is come to mock at form
harry the fifth is crowned / up vanity
down royal state / all you sage counsellors hence
and to the english court assemble now
from every region / apes of idleness
now neighbour confines purge you of your scum
have you a ruffian that will swear / drink / dance
revel the night / rob / murder and commit
the oldest sins the newest kind of ways?
be happy / he will trouble you no more
england shall double gild his treble guilt
england shall give him office / honour / might
for the fifth harry from curbed licence plucks
the muzzle of restraint and the wild dog
shall flesh his tooth on every innocent

o my poor kingdom / sick with civil blows
when that my care could not withhold thy riots
what wilt thou do when riot is thy care?
o thou wilt be a wilderness again
peopled with wolves / thy old inhabitants

PRINCE HARRY
o pardon me / my liege / but for my tears
i had forestalled this dear and deep rebuke
ere you with grief had spoke / and i had heard
the course of it so far / there is your crown
and he that wears the crown immortally
long guard it yours / if i affect it more
o let me in my present wildness die
and never live to show the incredulous world
the noble change that i have purposed
coming to look on you / thinking you dead
and dead almost / my liege / to think you were
i spake unto this crown as having sense
and thus upbraided it / i put it on my head
to try with it / as with an enemy
that had before my face / murdered my father
but if it did infect my blood with joy
or swell my thoughts to any strain of pride
let god forever keep it from my head

KING HENRY IV
o my son
god[452] put it in thy mind to take it hence
that thou mightst win the more thy father's love
pleading so wisely in excuse of it
come hither harry / sit thou by my bed
and hear i think the very final[453] counsel
that ever i shall breathe / god[454] knows my son
by what by-paths and indirect crooked ways
i met this crown / and i myself know well
how troublesome it sat upon my head
to thee it shall descend with better quiet
better opinion / better confirmation
for all the soil of the achievement goes
with me into the earth / it seemed in me

but as an honour snatched with boisterous hand
and i had many living to upbraid
my gain of it by their assistances
which daily grew to bloodshed / these bold fears
thou see'st / with peril / i have answered
for all my reign hath been but as a scene
acting that argument / and now my death
changes the mode[455] / for what in me was purchased
falls upon thee in a more fairer sort
so thou the garland wear'st successively
yet though thou stand'st more sure than i could do
thou art not firm enough / therefore my harry
be it thy course to busy giddy minds
with foreign quarrels / that action hence borne out
may waste the memory of the former days
more would i / but my lungs are wasted so
that strength of speech is utterly denied me
how i came by the crown / o god[456] forgive
and grant it may with you in true peace live

PRINCE HARRY
my gracious liege[457]
you won it / wore it / kept it / gave it me
then plain and right must my possession be

Enter Prince John, Prince Thomas and Warwick.

PRINCE JOHN
health / peace and happiness to my royal father

KING HENRY IV
thou bring'st me happiness / and peace / son john
but health / alack / with youthful wings is flown
from this bare withered trunk / upon thy sight
my worldly business comes unto its end
where's warwick? warwick[458]
doth any name particular belong
unto the lodging where i first did swoon?

WARWICK
'tis call'd jerusalem / my noble lord

KING HENRY IV
laud be to god[459] / even there my life must end
it hath been prophesied to me many years
i should not die but in jerusalem
which vainly i supposed the holy land
but bear me to that chamber / there i'll lie
in that jerusalem shall harry die

TWENTY-TWO[460]

Gloucestershire.

SHALLOW
nay / you shall see my[461] orchard / where in an arbour we will eat
a last year's pippin of my own grafting with a dish of caraways and
so forth / come cousin silence / and then to bed

DAVY
doth the man of war stay all night sir?

SHALLOW
yea davy / i will use him well / a friend in the court is better than a
penny in purse[462]

FALSTAFF
'fore god / you have here a goodly dwelling / and a rich

SHALLOW
barren / barren / barren / beggars all / beggars all sir john / marry /
good air / spread davy / spread davy / well said davy

FALSTAFF
this davy is your serving-man and your husbandman[463]

SHALLOW
a good varlet / a good varlet / a very good varlet sir john / by the
mass / i have drunk too much sack at supper / a good varlet / now
sit down / now sit down / come cousin

SILENCE (*sings*)
ah sirrah / quoth-a we shall
do nothing but eat and make good cheer
and praise <u>god</u>[464] for the merry year
when flesh is cheap and females dear
and lusty lads roam here and there
so merrily and ever among so merrily

FALSTAFF
there's a merry heart / good master silence / i'll give you a health
for that anon

SHALLOW
give master bardolph some wine davy / be merry master
bardolph / be merry

SILENCE (*sings*)
be merry / be merry / my wife has all
for women are shrews both short and tall
'tis merry in hall when beards wag all
and welcome merry shrove-tide
be merry be merry

FALSTAFF
i did not think master silence had been a man of this mettle

SILENCE
who i? i have been merry twice / and once ere now

DAVY
there's a dish of <u>russet apples</u>[465] for you

SHALLOW
davy

DAVY
a cup of wine sir?

SILENCE (*sings*)
a cup of wine that's brisk and fine
and drink unto the leman mine
and a merry heart lives long-a

FALSTAFF
well said master silence

SILENCE
an we shall be merry / now comes in the sweet o' the night

FALSTAFF
health and long life to you master silence

SILENCE (*sings*)
fill the cup and let it come
i'll pledge you a mile to the bottom

SHALLOW
honest bardolph / welcome / i'll drink a toast to master bardolph
and to all the cavaleros[466] about london

DAVY
i hope to see london once ere i die

BARDOLPH
i might see you there davy

SHALLOW
by the mass / you'll crack a quart together / ha / will you not
master bardolph?

BARDOLPH
yea sir

SHALLOW
by god / i thank thee / the knave will stick by thee / i can assure
thee that / he is true bred

BARDOLPH
and i'll stick by him sir

SHALLOW
why there spoke a king / lack nothing / be merry

Enter Shallow's Servant.

SHALLOW'S SERVANT[467]
an't please your worship / there's one come from the court with
news

Enter Pistol.

FALSTAFF
from the court / how now pistol

PISTOL
sir john / god save you

FALSTAFF
what wind blew you hither pistol?

PISTOL
not the ill wind which blows no man to good / sweet knight /
thou art now one of the greatest men in this[468] realm

FALSTAFF
i pray thee now deliver thy tidings[469]

SHALLOW
give me pardon sir / if sir you come with news from the court /
i am sir under the king in some authority

PISTOL
under which king?

SHALLOW
under king harry

PISTOL
harry the fourth? or fifth?

SHALLOW
harry the fourth

PISTOL
a foutre for thine office / sir john / thy tender lambkin now is king

FALSTAFF
what? is the old king dead?

PISTOL
as nail in door / henry the fifth's the man / <u>i speak the truth</u>[470]

FALSTAFF
away bardolph / saddle my horse / master robert shallow / choose
what office thou wilt in the land / 'tis thine / pistol / i will double-
charge thee with dignities

BARDOLPH
o joyful day / i would not take a <u>knighthood</u>[471] for my fortune

PISTOL
what / i do bring good news

FALSTAFF
carry master silence to bed / master shallow / my lord shallow /
be what thou wilt / get on thy boots / o sweet pistol / away
bardolph / i know the young king is sick for me / the laws of
england are at my commandment / blessed are they that have been
my friends / and woe to my lord chief justice

PISTOL
'where is the life that late i led?' say they
why here it is / welcome <u>these</u>[472] pleasant days

TWENTY-THREE[473]

LORD CHIEF JUSTICE
how doth the king?

WARWICK
exceeding well / his cares are now all ended

LORD CHIEF JUSTICE
i hope not dead

WARWICK
                he's walked the way of nature
and to our purposes he lives no more

LORD CHIEF JUSTICE
i would his majesty had called me with him

WARWICK
indeed i think the young king loves you not

LORD CHIEF JUSTICE
i know he doth not and do arm myself
to welcome the condition of the time
<u>o god</u>[474] / i fear all will be overturned

    Enter Prince John and Prince Thomas.

PRINCE JOHN
we meet like men that had forgot to speak

<u>WARWICK</u>[475]
well / peace be with him that hath made us heavy

LORD CHIEF JUSTICE
peace be with us lest we be heavier

PRINCE JOHN
<u>o good my lord / you have lost a friend indeed</u>[476]
though no man be assured what grace to find
you stand in coldest expectation
<u>and</u>[477] <u>you must now speak sir john falstaff fair</u>
<u>which swims against your stream of quality</u>[478]
<u>i am the sorrier / would 'twere otherwise</u>[479]

WARWICK
here comes the prince

    <u>*Enter Prince Harry, now King Henry V.*</u>[480]

LORD CHIEF JUSTICE
good morrow / and <u>god</u>[481] save your majesty

KING HENRY V
this new and gorgeous garment majesty
sits not so easy on me as you think
you all look strangely on me / and you most
you are / i think / assured i love you not

LORD CHIEF JUSTICE
i am assured if i be measured rightly
your majesty hath no just cause to hate me

KING HENRY V
no? how might a prince of my great hopes forget
so great indignities you laid upon me?
what / rate / rebuke and roughly send to prison
the immediate heir of england?

LORD CHIEF JUSTICE
i then did use the person of your father
the image of his power lay then in me
question your royal thoughts / make the case yours
be now the father / and propose a son
hear your own dignity so much profaned
see your most dreadful laws so loosely slighted
behold yourself so by a son disdained
and then imagine me taking your part
and / in your power / soft silencing your son
after this cold considerance sentence me
and / as you are a king / speak in your state
what i have done that misbecame my place
my person or my liege's sovereignty

KING HENRY V
you are right justice / and you weigh this well
and i do wish your honours may increase
till you do live to see a son of mine
offend you and obey you as i did
there is my hand
you shall be as a father to my youth
my voice shall sound as you do prompt mine ear
and / gentles[482] all / believe me / i beseech you
my father is gone wild into his grave
for in his tomb lie my affections
and with his spirits sadly i survive
our coronation done we will accite
our parliament / our court / and[483] all our state
in which you / father / shall have foremost hand[484]
and god[485] consigning to my good intents

no prince / nor peer / shall have just cause to say
<u>god</u>[486] shorten harry's happy life one day

TWENTY-FOUR[487]

Westminster.

FALSTAFF
stand here / by me / master <u>robert</u>[488] shallow / i will make the king
do you grace / do but mark the countenance that he will give me

PISTOL
<u>there roared the sea and trumpet-clangor sounds</u>[489] / <u>god</u>[490] bless
thy lungs good knight

FALSTAFF
come here pistol / stand behind me / o if i had had time to have
made new liveries / i would have <u>spent</u>[491] the thousand pound
i borrowed of you / but 'tis no matter / this poor show doth
better / this doth infer the zeal i had to see him

SHALLOW
it doth so

FALSTAFF
it shows my earnestness of affection

SHALLOW
it doth so

FALSTAFF
my devotion

SHALLOW
it doth / it doth / it doth

FALSTAFF
as it were / to <u>travel</u>[492] day and night / not to deliberate / not to
remember / not to have patience to <u>change</u>[493]

SHALLOW
it is <u>best</u>[494] / certain

FALSTAFF
but to stand stained with travel and sweating with desire to
see him / thinking of nothing else / putting all affairs <u>else</u>[495] in
oblivion / as if there were nothing else to be done but to see him

SHALLOW
'tis so indeed

Enter King Henry V, Lord Chief Justice, Warwick, and his train.

FALSTAFF
<u>god</u>[496] save thy grace / king hal / my royal hal / <u>god</u>[497] <u>save thee my
sweet boy</u>[498]

<u>WARWICK</u>[499]
my lord chief justice / speak to that vain man

LORD CHIEF JUSTICE
have you your wits? know you what 'tis you speak?

FALSTAFF
my king / my jove / i speak to thee my heart

KING HENRY V
i know thee not old man / fall to thy prayers
how ill white hairs become a fool and jester
i have long dreamed of such a kind of man
so surfeit-swelled / so old and so profane
but being awaked i do despise my dream
make less thy body hence and more thy grace
leave gormandising / know the grave doth gape
for thee thrice wider than for other men
reply not to me with a fool-born jest
presume not that i am the thing i was
for <u>god</u>[500] doth know / so shall the world perceive
that i have turned away my former self
so will i those that kept me company
when thou dost hear i am as i have been
approach me and you shall be as you were

the tutor and the feeder of my riots
till then i banish thee / on pain of death
as i have done the rest of my misleaders
not to come near our person by ten mile
and / as we hear you do reform yourselves
we will / according to your strengths and qualities
give you advancement / be it your charge my lord
to see performed the tenor of <u>our</u>[501] word

Exeunt King Henry V and his train.

FALSTAFF
master shallow / i owe you a thousand pound

SHALLOW
yea marry sir john / which i beseech you to let me have home with
me

FALSTAFF
that can hardly be master shallow / do not you grieve at this /
i shall be sent for in private to him / look you / he must seem thus
to the world / fear not your advancements / i will be the man that
shall make you great

SHALLOW
i cannot <u>well</u>[502] perceive how / i beseech you good sir john / let me
have five hundred of my thousand

FALSTAFF
sir / i will be as good as my word / this that you heard was but a
colour

SHALLOW
a colour that i fear you will die in sir john

FALSTAFF
fear no colours / go with me to dinner / come lieutenant pistol /
come bardolph / i shall be sent for soon / at night

[***][503]

PISTOL
bristle thy courage up / for falstaff he is dead

BARDOLPH
would i were with him / wheresoe'er he is / either in heaven or in
hell

MISTRESS QUICKLY
nay he's not in hell / he's in arthur's bosom / if ever man went to
arthur's bosom / he made a finer end and went away / an it had
been any christom child / he parted even just between twelve and
one / even at the turning o' the tide / for after i saw him fumble
with the sheets and play with flowers and smile upon his fingers'
ends / i knew there was but one way / for his nose was as sharp as
a pen and he babbled of green fields / 'how now sir john' quoth i /
'what man / be o' good cheer' / so he cried out 'god / god / god' /
three or four times / now i to comfort him bid him he should not
think of god / i hoped there was no need to trouble himself with
any such thoughts yet / so he[504] bade me lay more clothes on his
feet / i put my hand into the bed and felt them and they were as
cold as any stone / then i felt to his knees and they were as cold
as any stone[505] / and so upward and upward and all was as cold as
any stone

BARDOLPH
the king hath run bad humours on the knight / that's the even of
it[506]

PISTOL
ay[507] thou hast spoke the right[508] / the king has killed his heart[509]

[***][510]

PRINCE JOHN
i like this fair proceeding of the king's
he hath intent his wonted followers
shall all be very well provided for

LORD CHIEF JUSTICE
and so they are

PRINCE JOHN
the king hath called his parliament / my lord

LORD CHIEF JUSTICE
he hath

PRINCE JOHN
i will lay odds that ere this year expire
we bear our civil swords and native fire
as far as france / i heard a bird so sing
whose music to my thinking pleased the king
come / will you hence?

NOTES

Major versions

H1Q0 means *Henry IV Part 1*'s quarto 0 which features what modern editions consider 1.3.200-2.2.108, published in 1598

H1Q1 means *Henry IV Part 1*'s first issue of the quarto, published in 1598

H2Q1 means *Henry IV Part 2*'s first issue of the quarto in 1600

H2Q2 means *Henry IV Part 2*'s second issue of the quarto in 1600

F means The First Folio, published in 1623

Other editions and material used

H1Q2 means *Henry IV Part 1*'s quarto 2, published in 1599

H1Q3 means *Henry IV Part 1*'s quarto 3, published in 1604

H1Q4 means *Henry IV Part 1*'s quarto 4, published in 1608

H1Q5 means *Henry IV Part 1*'s quarto 5, published in 1613

H1Q6 means *Henry IV Part 1*'s quarto 6, published in 1622

H1Q7 means *Henry IV Part 1*'s quarto 7, published in 1632

H1Q8 means *Henry IV Part 1*'s quarto 8, published in 1639

Richard II, published in 1597

H5Q means *Henry V's* first quarto, published in 1600

The Famous Victories of Henry the Fifth by anonymous, published in 1598

F2 means The Second Folio, published in 1632

F3 means The Third Folio, published in 1663

F4 means The Fourth Folio, published in 1685

The Works of Shakespeare, ed. Alexander Pope, 6 vols (1723–5)

ENDNOTES

Text is from H1Q1 and H2Q2 unless otherwise stated

1   this scene is from *Henry IV Part 1*, 1.1
2   just this version ('broils' in H1Q1 F)
3   just this version ('in strands' in H1Q1 F)
4   just this version ('sepulcher of christ' in H1Q1 F)
5   from *Richard II*, 5.6
6   in H1Q F this line is spoken by Westmoreland
7   just this version ('loaden' in H1Q1 F)
8   just this version ('was' in H1Q1 F)
9   just this version ('leading' in H1Q1 F)
10   just this version (doesn't appear in H1Q1 F)
11   just this version ('this' in H1Q1 F)
12   in H1Q F this line is spoken by Westmoreland and King
     (Westmoreland speaks 'the gallant hotspur there / young harry
     percy' and King Henry IV speaks 'the earl of douglas [...] i shall
     have none')
13   just this version (doesn't appear in H1Q F)
14   just this version (doesn't appear in H1Q F)
15   just this version ('is discomfited' in H1Q F)
16   just this version ('two-and-twenty' in H1Q F)
17   just this version ('balked' in H1Q F)
18   just this version ('sir walter' in H1Q F)
19   just this version ('of' in H1Q F)
20   just this version ('was' in H1Q F)
21   just this version ('me' in H1Q F)
22   just this version ('i' in H1Q F)
23   in H1Q F, this line, spoken by Westmoreland, appears later (after
     King Henry IV's line 'to his own use he keeps and sends me word i
     shall have none but murdoch / earl of fife')
24   in H1Q F this line appears earlier (after King Henry IV's line 'the
     earl of douglas is discomfited / ten thousand bold scots / two and
     twenty knights / balked in their own blood / did sir walter see on
     holmedon's plains')
25   in H1Q F this line is spoken by Westmoreland
26   just this version (doesn't appear in H1Q F)

27   just this version (doesn't appear in H1Q F)
28   just this version ('for' in H1Q F)
29   in H1Q F this line appears earlier (after King Henry IV's line 'but
      i have sent for him to answer this' in response to Warwick's 'bristle
      up the crest of youth against your dignity')
30   this scene is from *Henry IV Part 1*, 1.2
31   just this version ('bawds' in H1Q F)
32   just this version ('on' in H1Q F)
33   just this version ('buff jerkin' in H1Q F)
34   just this version ('sweet' in H1Q F)
35   just this version ('judgest false' in H1Q F)
36   just this version ('thou shalt have the hanging of the thieves / and so
      become a rare hangman' in H1Q F)
37   just this version ('jumps' in H1Q F)
38   just this version ('gib cat' in H1Q F)
39   just this version ('lugged' in H1Q F)
40   from H1Q5 ('smiles' in H1Q1-4 and F)
41   from H1Q (doesn't appear in F)
42   from H1Q1 ('unto' in H1Q2-F)
43   just this version ('cried "stand!"' in H1Q F)
44   in H1Q1 F this line appears earlier (after Falstaff's line 'poins')
45   just this version ('madeira' in H1Q F)
46   just this version ('capon' in H1Q F)
47   just this version ('vizards' in H1Q F)
48   just this version ('you will' in H1Q F)
49   just this version ('nor' in H1Q F)
50   from H1Q ('maist thou have' in F)
51   just this version ('eastcheap' in H1Q F)
52   just this version ('will' in H1Q F)
53   just this version ('vizards' in H1Q F)
54   just this version ('doubt' in H1Q F)
55   just this version ('turned back' in H1Q F)
56   just this version ('eastcheap' in H1Q F)
57   just this version ('men' in H1Q F)
58   this scene is from *Henry IV Part 1*, 1.3
59   just this version ('holp' in H1Q F)
60   just this version ('see' in H1Q F)
61   just this version ('thine eye' in H1Q F)
62   just this version (doesn't appear in H1Q F)
63   just this version ('delivered' in H1Q F)
64   from H1Q ('was' in F)
65   from H1Q ('made me to answer' in F)
66   from H1Q1 ('this' in H1Q2-F)
67   just this version ('lord harry percy' in H1Q1 F)

68   just this version ('that earl of march' in H1Q F)
69   just this version ('great glendower' in H1Q F)
70   just this version ('with glendower' in H1Q F)
71   just this version ('an' in H1Q F)
72   just this version ('trembling' in H1Q F)
73   just this version (doesn't appear in H1Q F)
74   just this version ('gage them both' in H1Q F)
75   just this version ('that you are' in H1Q F)
76   just this version ('i'll' in H1Q F)
77   from H1Q1 ('waspe-tongued' in H1Q2-5, 'waspe-tongu'd' in F)
78   from H1Q ('insooth' in F)
79   just this version ('the douglas' son' in H1Q F)
80   just this version ('mean' in H1Q F)
81   just this version (doesn't appear in H1Q F)
82   just this version ('of york' in H1Q F)
83   this scene is from *Henry IV Part 1*, 2.2
84   just this version (doesn't appear in H1Q F)
85   this line is from from *Henry IV Part 1*, 2.1
86   just this version (doesn't appear in H1Q F)
87   just this version ('gummed velvet' in H1Q F)
88   just this version (doesn't appear in H1Q F)
89   just this version ('rascal' in H1Q F)
90   just this version ('break' in H1Q F)
91   just this version (doesn't appear in H1Q F)
92   just version ('an't' in H1Q F)
93   just this version ('as good a deed' in H1Q F)
94   just this version ('shall i be your ostler' in H1Q F)
95   from H1Q3-F (doesn't appear in H1Q1-2)
96   just this version ('peach' in H1Q F)
97   in H1Q1 F this line is spoken by a character called Gadshill
98   just this version (doesn't appear in H1Q1 F)
99   in H1Q1 F this line is spoken by Bardolph
100   in H1Q1 F this line is spoken by Gadshill
101   just this version ('vizards' in H1Q F)
102   just this version ('four' in H1Q F because there is another character
      called Gadshill in this scene)
103   in H1Q1 F this line is spoken by Peto
104   in H1Q1 F ('they' in H1Q2-Q6)
105   in H1Q1 F this line is spoken by Gadshill
106   just this version ('thou shalt' in H1Q F)
107   just this version ('gorbellied' in H1Q F)
108   just this version ('chuffs' in H1Q F)
109   just this version ('horse' in H1Q F)
110   just this version ('an' in H1Q F)

111   from H1Q1-2 ('sweares' in H1Q3-5)
112   this scene is from *Henry IV Part 2*, 3.1 (doesn't appear in H2Q)
113   from F ('pillowes' in H2Q2)
114   just this version ('deafing' in H2Q F)
115   this scene is from *Henry IV Part 1*, 2.4 unless specified otherwise
116   in H1Q F this line appears later (after Prince Harry's line 'i am no
       proud jack like falstaff / but a lad of mettle / a good boy by the lord
       / so they call me')
117   just this version ('drawers' in H1Q F)
118   from H1Q5 ('christen' H1Q1-4)
119   just this version (doesn't appear in H1Q F)
120   just this version (doesn't appear in H1Q F)
121   in H1Q1 F this line is spoken by Vintner
122   just this version (doesn't appear in H1Q F)
123   just this version (doesn't appear in H1Q F)
124   just this version ('of' in H1Q1 F)
125   just this version ('extant' in H1Q F)
126   just this version ('am i' in H1Q F)
127   just this version ('dagger of lath' in H1Q F)
128   from H1Q2-F ('not you' in H1Q1)
129   just this version ('i could' in H1Q F)
130   just this version ('four' in H1Q1 F where the fourth character is
       Gadshill)
131   just this version (doesn't appear in H1Q F)
132   just this version (doesn't appear in H1Q F)
133   just this version ('four' in H1Q F – see footnote 130)
134   just this version ('doublet' in H1Q F)
135   just this version ('sword' in H1Q F)
136   just this version ('ecce signum' in H1Q F)
137   just this version ('dealt' in H1Q F)
138   just this version ('four' in H1Q F – see footnote 130)
139   just this version ('they were bound' in H1Q F)
140   this line is spoken by Poins in H1Q5 F
141   just this version ('ward' in H1Q1-4, 'word' H1Q5 F)
142   just this version ('these hilts' in H1Q1 F)
143   just this version (doesn't appear in H1Q F)
144   just this version ('in' in H1Q F)
145   just this version ('an i were at the strappado / or all the racks' in
       H1Q F)
146   from H1Q3-5 F ('eel-skin' in H1Q1-2)
147   from H1Q1 F ('tried' in Q5)
148   just this version ('four' in H1Q F – see footnote 130)
149   just this version ('four' in H1Q F – see footnote 130)
150   just this version ('word' in H1Q F)

151   just this version ('bull calf' in H1Q F)
152   just this version (doesn't appear in H1Q F)
153   just this version ('glendower' in H1Q F)
154   just this version ('glendower' in H1Q F)
155   just this version ('a-horseback' in H1Q F)
156   just this version ('stolen away' in H1Q F)
157   from H1Q1-4 ('by night' in H1Q5-F)
158   just this version ('beard' in H1Q F)
159   just this version (doesn't appear in in H1Q F)
160   just this version (doesn't appear in in H1Q F)
161   from H1Q3-F ('so' in H1Q1-2)
162   just this version (doesn't appear in H1Q F)
163   just this version ('tun' in H1Q F)
164   just this version ('capon' in H1Q F)
165   from H1Q ('heaven' in F)
166   just this version ('in the' in H1Q F)
167   in H1Q F this line appears earlier (in response to Bardolph's line 'o
      my lord / the sheriff with a most monstrous watch is at the door'
      which comes after 'a loud knocking')
168   in H1Q F this line appears earlier (after 'a loud knocking')
169   in H1Q F this line appears earlier (after Mistress Quickly's line 'the
      sheriff and all the watch are at the door / they are come to search
      the house / shall i let them in')
170   from *The Famous Victories of Henry V*, Scene 4
171   just this version (doesn't appear in H1Q F or *The Famous Victories of
      Henry V*)
172   in H1Q F this line is spoken by Sheriff
173   in H1Q F this line is spoken by Sheriff
174   in H1Q F this line is spoken by Sheriff
175   the following section, until the exit of the Lord Chief Justice and
      Carrier, is from *The Famous Victories of Henry V*, Scene 4
176   just this version ('rascal' in H1Q F)
177   just this version (doesn't appear in H1Q F)
178   from H1Q1-3 ('be they' in H1Q4-F)
179   just this version ('capon' in H1Q F)
180   just this version ('ob' in H1Q F)
181   this scene is from *Henry IV Part 1*, 3.2
182   from H1Q ('heaven' in F)
183   from H1Q1 F ('the' in H1Q2-Q4)
184   just this version ('marked' in H1Q F)
185   just this version ('he' in H1Q F)
186   just this version ('swaddling' in H1Q1, 'swathing' in H1Q4-F)
187   just this version ('percy' in H1Q F)
188   just this version ('the archbishop's grace of york' in H1Q F)

189   just this version ('are up' in H1Q F)
190   from H1Q ('heaven' in F)
191   just this version ('percy's' in H1Q F)
192   just this version ('hath' in H1Q F)
193   this scene is from *Henry IV Part 1*, 3.3
194   just this version ('diced' in H1Q F)
195   just this version ('bawdy-house' in H1Q F)
196   just this version ('the tithe of' in H1Q F)
197   just this version ('dowlas, filthy dowlas' in H1Q F)
198   from H1Q ('pounds' in F)
199   just this version ('denier' in H1Q F)
200   just this version (''sblood an he were here' in H1Q F)
201   just this version (in H1Q F, Prince Harry enters 'with Peto')
202   from H1Q ('let' in F)
203   just this version ('charge of foot' in H1Q F)
204   just this version ('furniture' in H1Q F)
205   just this version ('percy' in H1Q F)
206   from H1Q1-3 F ('they or we' in H1Q4-Q5)
207   this scene is comprised of *Henry IV Part 1*, 2.3 and 4.3
208   just this version (doesn't appear in H1Q F)
209   from H1Q1 ('beds' H1Q2-F)
210   just this version (doesn't appear in H1Q F)
211   just this version (doesn't appear in H1Q F)
212   just this version ('afoot' in H1Q F)
213   from H1Q ('thou speakst' in F)
214   from H1Q ('whether' in F)
215   just this version (doesn't appear in H1Q F)
216   the rest of this scene is from *Henry IV Part 1*, 4.3
217   just this version ('now' in H1Q F)
218   just this version ('he presently' in H1Q F)
219   just this version ('absent' in H1Q F)
220   just this version (doesn't appear in H1Q F)
221   from H1Q5-F ('mine' in H1Q1-4)
222   from H1Q ('heaven' in F)
223   this scene is from *Henry IV Part 1*, 4.2
224   just this version ('soused gurnet' in H1Q F)
225   just this version ('the King's press' in H1Q F)
226   just this version ('press me' in H1Q F)
227   just this version (doesn't appear in H1Q F)
228   just this version ('pressed me' in H1Q F)
229   just this version ('dishonourable' in H1Q F)
230   just this version ('feazed ancient' in H1Q F)
231   just this version ('gibbets' in H1Q F)
232   just this version ('pressed' in H1Q F)

233 in H1Q F this line appears earlier (after Falstaff's line 'that you would think that i had a hundred and fifty tattered prodigals lately come from swine-keeping / from eating draff and husks')
234 in H1Q F this line is spoken by Westmoreland
235 just this version ('looks' in H1Q F)
236 in H1Q F this line is spoken by Westmoreland
237 just this version ('percy' in H1Q F)
238 just this version ('fits' in H1Q F)
239 this scene is from *Henry IV Part 1*, 4.1
240 from H1Q ('heaven' in F)
241 just this version ('letters from him' in H1Q F which is in response to Messenger's line 'these letters come from your father')
242 just this version ('did' in H1Q F)
243 just this version ('some' in H1Q F)
244 in H1Q F this line appears earlier in Worcester's speech (after 'the quality and hair of our attempt brooks no division')
245 from ('at' in H1Q5-F)
246 just this version ('my cousin' in H1Q1 F)
247 just this version ('the earl of westmoreland' in H1Q1 F)
248 from H1Q1-2 ('hath' in H1Q3-F)
249 just this version ('let them come' in H1Q F)
250 just this version ('glendower' in H1Q F)
251 just this version ('glendower' in H1Q F)
252 in H1Q1 F these lines appear in a later scene (*Henry IV Part 1*, 5.2)
253 this scene is from *Henry IV Part 1*, 5.1
254 from H1Q1 ('busky' in H1Q2-F)
255 from H1Q1 F ('the' in H1Q3)
256 just this version ('it was' in H1Q F)
257 just this version ('to gripe the general sway' in H1Q F)
258 just this version ('forgot' in H1Q F)
259 just this version ('troth' in H1Q F)
260 just this version (doesn't appear in H1Q F)
261 in H1Q F this line appears earlier (in response to the King's 'nor moody beggars starving for a time of pellmell havoc and confusion')
262 just this version ('and' in H1Q F)
263 just this version ('on' in H1Q F)
264 from H1Q ('heaven' in F)
265 just this version ('bestride' in H1Q F)
266 from H1Q ('heaven' in F)
267 just this version (in H1Q F Prince Harry exits after 'why thou owest god a death')
268 just this version ('that' in H1Q F)
269 this scene is comprised of *Henry IV Part 1*, 5.3, 5.4 and 5.5 unless specified otherwise

270   this section is from *Henry IV Part 1*, 5.3
271   from H1Q5-F ('a yielder' in H1Q1-4)
272   just this version ('this' in H1Q F)
273   just this version ('a gallant knight he was / his name was blunt' in H1Q F)
274   from H1Q ('heaven' in F)
275   this section is from *Henry IV Part 1*, 5.4
276   from F ('and' in H1Q)
277   in H1Q F this line appears earlier (at top of scene)
278   from H1Q ('heaven' in F)
279   from H1Q1-3 ('to' in H1Q4-F)
280   in H1Q F this line is spoken by Westmoreland and said earlier (in response to King Henry IV's 'my lord of Westmoreland lead him to his tent')
281   from H1Q ('heaven' in F)
282   just this version (in H1Q F Falstaff enters after Hostpur's line 'i can no longer brook thy vanities')
283   just this version ('harry monmouth' in H1Q F)
284   just this version ('see' in H1Q F)
285   from F ('now' in H1Q)
286   from H1Q ('heaven' in F)
287   from H1Q1 ('earth' in H1Q2-F)
288   from H1Q7 ('the dead' in H1Q1-6 F)
289   from H1Q1 F ('faire' in H1Q2-5)
290   just this version ('powder' in H1Q F)
291   from H1Q1-4 ('the' Q5-F)
292   just this version ('take' in H1Q F)
293   just this version ('bring' in H1Q F)
294   these lines are from *Henry IV Part 2*, 4.2
295   these lines are from *Henry IV Part 2*, 4.2
296   this section is from *Henry IV Part 1*, 5.5
297   in H1Q F this line is spoken by Prince Harry in *Henry IV Part 1*, 5.4
298   from H1Q1-4 ('way' in H1Q5-F)
299   just this version (doesn't appear in H1Q F)
300   this scene is from *Henry IV Part 2*, 4.2
301   just this version ('sherris' in H2Q F)
302   from H2Q ('his' in F)
303   just this version ('sherris' in H2Q F)
304   just this version ('sherris' in H2Q F)
305   this scene is from *Henry IV Part 2*, 2.3
306   from H2Q ('heavens' in F)
307   from H2Q ('when' in F)
308   just this version ('percy' in H2Q F)

309   this scene is from *Henry IV Part 2*, 1.2
310   just this version ('that committed the prince for striking him about bardolph' in H2Q F)
311   in H2Q F this line is spoken by Servant
312   just this version ('the disease' in H2Q F)
313   just this version ('costermongers' in H2Q F)
314   just this version ('a white head' in H2Q F)
315   from H2Q ('heaven' in F)
316   from H2Q ('heaven' in F)
317   just this version ('lord john of lancaster against the archbishop' in H2Q F)
318   from H2Q ('heaven' in F)
319   the rest of this scene is from *Henry IV Part 2*, 2.1
320   in H2Q F this line is spoken by Fang
321   just this version ('exion' in H2Q F)
322   just this version ('god's officers and the king' in H2Q F)
323   in H2Q F this line is spoken by Page
324   just this version ('more than' in H2Q F)
325   from F ('wheeson' in H2Q)
326   just this version ('and call' in H2Q F)
327   just this version ('green' in H2Q F)
328   from H2Q ('familiar' in F)
329   just this version ('gower' in H2Q F)
330   in H2Q F this line is spoken by Gower
331   just this version ('an 't' in H2Q F)
332   just this version ('draw' in H2Q F)
333   in H2Q F this appears earlier (at the top of Falstaff's line)
334   just this version ('twenty nobles' in H2Q F)
335   just this version ('will' in H2Q F)
336   in H2Q F this line appears earlier (after Falstaff's line 'will i live')
337   from H2Q ('bitter' in F)
338   from F ('tonight' in H2Q)
339   in H2Q F this line is spoken by Gower
340   just this version ('basingstoke' in F and 'billingsgate' in H2Q)
341   in H2Q F this line is spoken by Gower
342   just this version ('my lord' in H2Q F)
343   just this version ('archbishop' in H2Q F)
344   just this version ('counties' in Q, 'countries' in F)
345   just this version ('gower' in H2Q F)
346   just this version ('gower' in H2Q F)
347   this scene is from *Henry IV Part 1*, 2.2
348   from H2Q ('trust me' in F)
349   just this version (doesn't appear in H2Q F)
350   from F4 ('vildly' in H2Q and 'vildely' in F1-3)

351   just this version ('meet' in H2Q F)
352   just this version ('hardly' in H2Q F)
353   just this version ('martlemas' in H2Q F)
354   just this version ('lo' in H2Q F)
355   in H2Q F this line is spoken by Prince Harry
356   just this version ('frank' in H2Q F)
357   just this version (doesn't appear in H2Q F)
358   just this version ('road' in H2Q F)
359   just this version ('way' in H2Q F)
360   just this version ('jerkins' in H2Q F)
361   from H2Q ('like' in F)
362   just this version ('drawers' in H2Q F)
363   in H2Q F this line comes earlier (after Prince Harry's line 'that's to make him eat twenty of his words' in response to Poins 'my lord / i'll steep this letter in sack and make him eat it')
364   from H2Q ('may the wench have' in F)
365   this scene is from *Henry IV Part 2*, 2.4
366   in H2Q F this line is spoken by First Drawer
367   just this version ('applejohn' in H2Q F)
368   just this version ('sect' in H2Q F)
369   just this version ('rascal' in H2Q F)
370   just this version ('hogshead' in H2Q F)
371   in H2Q F this line is spoken by First Drawer
372   from H2Q ('amongst' in F)
373   just this version ('feel / masters / how i shake / look you' in H2Q2 F)
374   just this version ('dorothy' in H2Q2 F)
375   just this version ('dorothy' in H2Q2 F)
376   in H2Q F this line appears earlier (after Doll's line 'away you cut purse rascal')
377   just this version ('ancient' in H2Q2 F)
378   in H2Q F this line is said by Page
379   just this version (doesn't appear in H2Q F)
380   just this version ('quoit' in H2Q F)
381   in H2Q2 F this line appears earlier (after Pistol's line 'thrust him downstairs / know we not galloway nags')
382   just this version ('methought a' made' in H2Q2 F)
383   just this version ('foining' in H2Q2 F)
384   just this version ('pantler' in H2Q F)
385   just this version ('ha' in H2Q F)
386   just this version ('quoits' in H2Q F)
387   just this version ('the prince' in H2Q F)
388   just this version ('nave of a wheel' in H2Q F)
389   just this version ('where' in H2Q F)
390   just this version ('poll' in H2Q F)

391   in H2Q F this appears later (after Falstaff's 'kiss me Doll')
392   just this version ('busses' in H2Q F)
393   just this version ('kirtle' in H2Q F)
394   in H2Q F this line is spoken by Hal and Poins
395   from H2Q2 ('heaven' in F)
396   from F (doesn't appear in H2Q F)
397   just this version (doesn't appear in H2Q F)
398   just this version ('by' in H2Q F)
399   just this version ('not' in H2Q F)
400   just this version ('pantler' in H2Q F)
401   just this version ('presently' in H2Q F)
402   just this version ('a dozen captains' in H2Q F)
403   in H2Q F this line is spoken by Bardolph
404   just this version ('cloak' in H2Q F)
405   just this version (doesn't appear in H2Q F)
406   just this version (doesn't appear in H2Q F)
407   this scene is from *Henry IV Part 2*, 3.1 (doesn't appear in H2Q)
408   just this version ('then' in H2Q F)
409   just this version ('cooled' in H2Q F)
410   just this version ('heaven' in F)
411   just this version ('but which of you was by' in H2Q F)
412   just this version ('heaven' in F)
413   just this version ('bishop and' in H2Q F)
414   from H2Q ('life' in F)
415   this scene is from *Henry IV Part 2*, 3.2
416   from *The Works of Shakespeare*, ed. Alexander Pope ('cotsole' in H2Q)
417   from H2Q ('saw' in F)
418   from H2Q ('oh' in F)
419   from H2Q (doesn't appear in F)
420   from F ('dooble' in H2Q)
421   from F ('a' in H2Q)
422   from F ('a' in H2Q)
423   from F ('dooble' in H2Q)
424   just this version (doesn't appear in H2Q F)
425   from F ('trust me' in H2Q)
426   from F ('like' in H2Q)
427   just this version (doesn't appear in H2Q F)
428   just this version ('soccard' in H2Q, 'sure-card' in F)
429   in H2Q this line appears later (after Shallow's line 'i shall never see such a fellow')
430   in H2Q F this line appears later (after Shallow's line 'here is two more called than your number you must have but four here / sir')
431   from H2Q ('it was' in F)

432   from H2Q F ('oh' in F)
433   this line is from *Henry IV Part 2*, 5.1
434   this scene is from *Henry IV Part 2*, 4.3
435   just this version ('humphrey / my son of gloucester / where is the prince your brother?' in H2Q F)
436   just this version (originally 'prince humphrey' in H2Q F)
437   just this version ('him / thomas?' in H2Q F)
438   just this version ('who's here' in H2Q F)
439   just this version ('westmoreland' in H2Q F)
440   in H2Q F this line is spoken by Westmoreland (after Westmoreland's line 'health to my sovereign and new happiness added to that that i am to deliver'
441   just this version (doesn't appear in H2Q F)
442   in H2Q F this line is spoken by Prince Humphrey
443   in H2Q F this line is spoken by Westmoreland
444   just this version ('to' in H2Q F)
445   in H2Q F this line is spoken by Prince Humphrey
446   in H2Q F this line is spoken by Prince Humphrey
447   just this version ('rigol' in H2Q F)
448   just this version ('from' in H2Q F)
449   just this version ('lo' in H2Q F)
450   just this version ('where' in H2Q F)
451   from H2Q ('heaven' in F)
452   from H2Q ('heaven' in F)
453   just this version ('latest' in H2Q F)
454   from H2Q ('heaven' in F)
455   from F3-4 ('mood' in H2Q F1-F2)
456   from H2Q ('heaven' in F)
457   from F (doesn't appear in H2Q)
458   just this version (doesn't appear in H2Q F)
459   from H2Q ('heaven' in F)
460   this scene is from *Henry IV Part 2*, 5.3 unless specified otherwise
461   from H2Q ('mine' in F)
462   these lines are from *Henry IV Part 2*, 5.2
463   just this version ('husband' in H2Q F)
464   from H2Q ('heaven' in F)
465   just this version ('leather-coats' in H2Q F)
466   from F ('cabileros' in H2Q)
467   in H2Q F this line is spoken by Davy
468   from H2Q ('the' in F)
469   just this version ('them like a man of this world' in H2Q F)
470   just this version ('the things i speak are just' in H2Q F)
471   from F ('knight' in H2Q)
472   from H2Q ('those' in F)

473   this scene is from *Henry IV Part 2*, 5.2
474   from H2Q ('alas' in F)
475   in H2Q F this line is spoken by Prince John (after Warwick's line 'we do remember / but our argument is all too heavy to admit much talk')
476   in H2Q F this line is spoken by Prince Humphrey
477   just this version ('well' in H2Q F)
478   in H2Q F this line is spoken by Prince Thomas
479   in H2Q F this line comes earlier (after Prince John's line 'you stand in coldest expectation')
480   just this version (doesn't appear in H2Q F)
481   from H2Q ('heaven' in F)
482   just this version ('princes' in H2Q F)
483   just this version ('as i before remembered' in H2Q F)
484   in H2Q F this line appears earlier (after Prince Harry's line 'that war / or peace / or both at once / may be as things acquainted and familiar to us')
485   from H2Q ('heaven' in F)
486   from H2Q ('heaven' in F)
487   this scene is from *Henry IV Part 2*, 5.5 unless specified otherwise
488   from F (doesn't appear in H2Q)
489   in H2Q F this appears later (after Falstaff's line 'i will deliver her')
490   from H2Q (doesn't appear in F)
491   just this version ('bestowed' in H2Q F)
492   just this version ('ride' in H2Q F)
493   just this version ('shift me' in H2Q F)
494   from H2Q ('most' in F)
495   from H2Q (doesn't appear in F)
496   from H2Q (doesn't appear in F)
497   from H2Q (doesn't appear in F)
498   in H2Q F this line appears later (after Pistol's line 'the heavens thee guard and keep / most royal imp of fame')
499   in H2Q F this line is spoken by King Henry V
500   from H2Q ('heaven' in F)
501   from F ('my' in H2Q)
502   from F (doesn't appear in H2Q)
503   this section is from *Henry V*, 2.3
504   just this version ('a' in *Henry V*)
505   from H5Q (doesn't appear in F)
506   this line is from *Henry V*, 2.1 and is spoken by Nym
507   just this version ('nym' in *Henry V*)
508   this line is from *Henry V*, 2.1
509   appears earlier in *Henry V*, 2.1 and is spoken by Mistress Quickly
510   this section is from *Henry IV Part 2*, 5.5

www.nickhernbooks.co.uk

facebook.com/nickhernbooks

twitter.com/nickhernbooks